T0196336

AT THE
CROSSROADS OF JUSTICE

My Lai and Son Thang—
American Atrocities in Vietnam

Paul J. Noto

iUniverse, Inc.
Bloomington

At the Crossroads of Justice
My Lai and Son Thang—American Atrocities in Vietnam

iUniverse books may be ordered through booksellers or by contacting:

iUniverse
1663 Liberty Drive
Bloomington, IN 47403
www.iuniverse.com
1-800-Authors (1-800-288-4677)

Because of the dynamic nature of the Internet, any Web addresses or links contained in this book may have changed since publication and may no longer be valid. The views expressed in this work are solely those of the author and do not necessarily reflect the views of the publisher, and the publisher hereby disclaims any responsibility for them.

Any people depicted in stock imagery provided by Thinkstock are models, and such images are being used for illustrative purposes only.

Certain stock imagery © Thinkstock.

ISBN: 978-1-4620-5012-3 (sc)
ISBN: 978-1-4620-5014-7 (hc)
ISBN: 978-1-4620-5013-0 (e)

Library of Congress Control Number: 2011915127

Printed in the United States of America

iUniverse rev. date: 10/14/2011

"Nearly all men can stand adversity, but if you want to test a man's character, give him power."
Abraham Lincoln

"Whatever America hopes to bring to pass in the world must first come to pass in the heart of America."
Dwight D. Eisenhower

For Jennifer, Melissa, and Heather

CONTENTS

INTRODUCTION

The twentieth century is often referred to as the American century. It was the century during which the United States emerged as a world power both economically and militarily. Having asserted itself as a military power at the end of the nineteenth century with its convincing victory in the Spanish-American War, the United States established itself as a brash and daring competitor to the European powers that had dominated world affairs since 1815. After the fall of Napoleon, the monarchies of Europe established a series of agreements among the world's dominant powers that maintained relative peace in the world from 1815 until the outbreak of World War I in 1914.

Having provided the decisive blow to the Germans to win World War I and having carried the Allies to victory in World War II, the United States became the predominant world power. Subsequently, challenged solely by the Soviet Union—the only other nuclear power— the United States established a series of doctrines that set forth an ambitious policy to oppose the spread of Communism anywhere in the world. This opposition to Communism included diplomatic, economic, and military initiatives. The world had become a bipolar landscape where countries were often forced to choose between the two main Cold War powers.

Against this backdrop of Cold War drama, the world was

experiencing dramatic social change. The advancement of women's rights and civil rights, plus the disenchantment of American youth in reaction to stagnant economies and high unemployment, led to unrest and turmoil in the West. By 1968 the United States was mired in a bloody war in Vietnam, which had already cost the United States over thirty thousand casualties with no end to the conflict in sight. The war exacerbated existing divisions over civil rights and social change to the point where the United States was more divided than at any time since the Civil War.

That year, 1968, was one of the most significant years in the American century, as it witnessed some of the most tumultuous events of American history. One such event occurred in January during the aforementioned conflict overseas. The Viet Cong launched an ambitious series of attacks on hundreds of towns, villages, and cities throughout South Vietnam. The offensive took place on the lunar New Year, taking the United States and South Vietnamese forces by surprise. Known as the Tet Offensive, the Viet Cong's large-scale, simultaneous attacks underscored their ability to surprise the American and South Vietnamese forces and undermined the premise that the United States was succeeding in its military effort. While a failure by military standards, Tet was a public relations bonanza for the Viet Cong, as millions of Americans saw video of the fighting for the first time. American television reporters embedded in South Vietnam were able to capture graphic images of the battles, which began to turn public opinion against the war.

The presidential primary season was under way, with President Lyndon Baines Johnson facing a strong challenge from antiwar senator Eugene McCarthy of Minnesota. Hampered by his unpopular Vietnam strategy, Johnson barely beat McCarthy in the New Hampshire primary. Unable to attract much support for his war policy, in March he withdrew from the race, less than four years after winning the presidency by the largest margin in history.

The civil rights movement, which had gained momentum, generated violent confrontations in many parts of the country. In April, Reverend Martin Luther King, Jr., was assassinated in Memphis, Tennessee. King was a charismatic and telegenic leader who had enormously advanced the civil rights cause. His death spawned riots and violent protests in many American cities.

Two months later Senator Robert F. Kennedy, the brother of the late President John F. Kennedy, was gunned down after winning the California presidential primary. Robert Kennedy had been an inspirational leader, an opponent of the Vietnam War, and a vocal supporter of the civil rights movement. He had become a spokesperson for the underprivileged, promising new federal initiatives to help the poor and eradicate hunger in America.

Throughout that year, student protests erupted at college campuses all over the country. Unrest and turmoil were the norm in America. To many, it seemed as if America was coming apart at the seams.

It is fitting that during this extraordinary year in American history one of the most significant tragedies in US military history occurred in Vietnam. The My Lai massacre took place on March 16, 1968, far from the protests in America but very much symbolic of the confusion, ambivalence, and hatred generated by this war. Less than two years later, a group of United States Marines perpetrated a second incident, at Son Thang.

To many, these incidents were an indictment of the war itself, a reflection of the poor leadership, failed policy, and inept execution of an ill-defined war plan. The soldiers were simply scapegoats for a bigger failure imposed on the American people by foolish and arrogant political leaders. Or was there more to the story that prompted American soldiers to engage in a killing frenzy that ended in deaths of over five hundred South Vietnamese civilians?

Here I examine these two incidents, first explaining the process by which soldiers are trained to kill their fellow humans, and then analyzing what happened when the specific incidents took place and how the military handled them. Furthermore, this work addresses the legal issues raised in the prosecution and defense of all involved and how the outcomes affected the US military. Ultimately this book tries to answer the question of why these incidents occurred and who was ultimately responsible for them.

At the time of this writing, it is now forty-three years since My Lai, and many of the soldiers who participated in the incident are still alive. The United States is currently involved in two wars. Afghanistan and Iraq are countries with striking similarities to Vietnam in the 1960s. It is important, given America's military commitment to these conflicts, that we reexamine the massacres in Vietnam to ensure that similar incidents do not happen again.

CHAPTER 1
Why Kill?

IN 1991 a coalition of countries sent troops to the Persian Gulf to commence military action against Iraq, driving the Iraqi army out of Kuwait. The single largest contingent of coalition forces was from the United States. Major General Ronald Griffith, commander of the First Armored Division, United States Army, addressed his men as they were about to go to battle and exhorted them: "No My Lai's in this Division—do you hear me!"[1]

What is it about the term *My Lai* that makes military commanders so fearful, even though the event referred to took place more than a generation ago? Most of Major General Griffith's troops were not even born when My Lai took place, yet he and many other military commanders made a point of reminding their men of the event's importance.

Atrocities in war are nothing new. In 1864 at Sand Creek, Colorado, six hundred Cheyenne Indians were gathered to camp for the winter. Without warning or provocation US soldiers under the command of

---

1   William G. Eckhardt. "My Lai: An American Tragedy." 2000.

Colonel John Chivington charged the camp and murdered one-third of the Indians, mostly women and children. In the Philippines from 1899 to 1902 US troops waged a bloody conflict with Filipinos, whom they called "gooks," who were resisting American colonization. Part of the American strategy was to torture captives and destroy villages, including killing all of the villages' inhabitants.[2] World War II saw many atrocities on both sides. Besides the obvious ethnic cleansing carried out by the Germans and Japanese, the Allies firebombed entire cities in those countries in a deliberate attempt to kill civilians and undermine support for the war effort.

So why, in light of past military policy allowing for the killing of civilians to advance the war effort, do My Lai and Son Thang remain so problematic for the American psyche? American exceptionalism is a powerful concept. To think American soldiers broke down and fell victim to committing an atrocity is to cling to that myth of American exceptionalism. In Anderson's book on My Lai, Tim O'Brien is quoted, "Evil has no place ... in our national mythology."[3]

In answering the question above one has to be mindful of an admonition by World War II historian Stephen E. Ambrose, who argues that it is difficult to judge someone's actions when one has not been in combat themselves. Combat is the most extreme experience a human being can go through. There is little in civilian life to compare to it, and for the vast majority of people combat is an alien concept.

If you were born between 1890 and 1900 and you were white, you were almost certain to be in combat. If you were born in Europe in the 1830s and were white, you were almost certain not to be in combat. But combat is an experience most people simply don't have. Could I stand

---

2   David L. Anderson. *Facing My Lai: Moving Beyond the Massacre.* Lawrence, Kansas: University Press of Kansas, 1998, p. 113.

3   Anderson, p. 113.

up to the rigors of combat? Could I kill? Could I charge an enemy who is trying to kill me? Would I be brave? Would I be cowardly? Would I hide? Would I lead? Very few people get to answer these questions. We must always keep that in mind when dealing with things that happen in and around combat.[4]

To address those questions in the broader context of warfare, it is important to appreciate how armies train soldiers to kill. There is a powerful, innate human resistance to killing a member of one's own species.

Brigadier General S. L. A. Marshall was a US Army historian and became the official US historian of the European theatre of operations in World War II. He and his team interviewed thousands of soldiers who had served in both Europe and the Pacific. These interviews took place shortly after the soldiers had been in close combat with German or Japanese troops. The results were consistently the same: only 15 to 20 percent of the American riflemen in combat situations would fire at the enemy. Those who did not fire, did not run or hide, and in many cases they were willing to risk great danger to rescue wounded comrades, get ammunition, or run messages. But they simply would not fire their weapons at the enemy, even when faced with repeated banzai charges.[5] Ample supporting evidence indicates that Marshall's observations are applicable not only to American soldiers or even to all soldiers within World War II alone. There is compelling data to indicate that this singular lack of enthusiasm for killing one's fellow man has existed throughout military history.[6]

The origin of man's resistance to killing is unclear, although it may stem from the simple notion that all people understand at some gut level

---

4   Anderson, p. 109.

5   David Grossman. *On Killing: The Psychological Cost of Learning to Kill in War and Society.* Boston: Little, Brown and Company, 1995, pp. 3–4.

6   Grossman, p. 16.

that all of humanity is inextricably interdependent and that to harm any part is to harm the whole. The Roman emperor Marcus Aurelius wrote almost two millennia ago, "Every individual dispensation is one of the causes of the prosperity, success and even survival of that which administers the universe. To break off any particle, no matter how small, from the continuous concatenation—whether of causes or of other elements—is to injure the whole."[7]

Killing a fellow human can create a terrible burden on the human psyche. Tim O'Brien describes his feelings twenty years after his tour of Vietnam: "Even now I haven't finished sorting it out. Sometimes I forgive myself, other times I don't. In the ordinary hours of life I try not to dwell on it, but now sitting alone in a room, I'll look up and see the young man step out of the morning fog. I'll watch him walk toward me, his shoulders slightly stooped, his head cocked to the side, and he'll pass within a few yards of me and suddenly smile at some secret thought and then continue up the trail to where it bends back into the fog."[8]

Grossman points out that the resistance to killing is so great that it is often sufficient to overcome the cumulative influences of the instinct for self-preservation and the coercive forces of leadership and peer pressure. William Manchester, historian and US Marine veteran, felt remorse and shame after his close-range encounter and killing of a Japanese soldier. "I can remember whispering foolishly, 'I'm sorry' and then just throwing up … I threw up all over myself. It was a betrayal of what I'd been taught since a child."[9]

While popular culture tends to romanticize killing during wartime, the reality is much different. A person's true, visceral response to killing

---

7   Grossman, p. 39.

8   Tim O'Brien. *The Things They Carried*. New York: Mariner Books, 1990, p. 128.

9   Grossman, p. 87.

is far different than that depicted in movies or television. Grossman reports several veterans' reactions to the gruesomeness of killing.

"Killing is the worst thing that one man can do to another man … It's the last thing that should happen anywhere."—Israeli lieutenant

"I reproached myself as a destroyer. An indescribable uneasiness came over me, I almost felt like a criminal."—Napoleonic-era British soldier

"I fired again and somehow got him in the head. There was so much blood … I vomited, until the rest of the boys came up."—Israeli Six Day War veteran

"And I froze, 'cos it was boy, I would say between the ages of twelve and fourteen. When he turned at me and looked, all of a sudden he turned his whole body and pointed his automatic weapon at me. I just opened up, fired the whole twenty rounds right at the kid, and he just laid there. I dropped my weapon and cried."—US Special Forces officer and Vietnam veteran[10]

Ideology often plays little role in the motivation for a soldier to fight. Certainly ideology is important as much to motivate the public to support a war as it is to motivate soldiers to fight. The American Civil War was initially said to be fought to preserve the Union but gradually morphed into being called a war to end slavery. The shift in philosophy was necessary to shore up weakening support for the war effort in the Northern antislavery states. From an American standpoint,

---

10   Grossman, p. 87.

World War I was supposed to be the war to end all wars, and World War II was waged to avenge the attack on Pearl Harbor and to prevent the spread of totalitarianism. The ideology provides the intellectual and emotional foundation for the war effort, but the combat soldier often has a different view of what he is fighting for.

Group pressures and other motivating factors play an even larger role in battlefield motivation. Regard for their comrades, respect for their leaders, concern for their own reputation, and an urge to contribute to the success of the group are far more powerful motivators than ideology.

"This may sound strange but there is a love relationship that is nurtured in combat because the man next to you—you're depending on him for the most important thing you have—your life, and if he lets you down you're either maimed or killed … Your life is in his hands, you trust that person with the most valuable thing you have."—John Early, Vietnam veteran and ex-Rhodesian mercenary[11]

This bonding is so intense that it is fear of failing these comrades that preoccupies most combatants. The guilt and trauma associated with failing to fully support men who are bonded with friendship and camaraderie on this magnitude is profoundly intense.[12]

In Vietnam this concept was particularly significant. Colonel Mathew Parrish, an Army psychiatrist, observed, "The soldier in Vietnam doesn't fight for God and country. He fights for his company and his platoon. He fires his weapon for his team or squad or platoon or company too. The soldier fires his weapon because he feels his buddy

---

11   Grossman, p. 89.
12   Grossman, p. 89.

expects him to fire his weapon. He cannot let his buddy down. He cannot let the team down."[13]

Most people know that killing is an unnatural act, yet we continue to look for ways to explain the mechanisms by which killing, sometimes on a large scale, can be justified in war. In 1945 over one hundred thousand Germans, mostly civilians, were killed in the Dresden air raid. The Tokyo firebombings took two hundred and twenty-five thousand Japanese civilian lives. The Germans killed six million Jews, mostly by poison gas and firing squads. Yet when we think of those bombed in Dresden or Tokyo there is no feeling of disgust for the deed as there is when considering the Holocaust. Lieutenant Colonel Grossman points out the qualitative distinction we make in the eyes of those who suffered: the survivors of Auschwitz were personally traumatized by criminals and suffered lifelong psychological damage from their experiences, whereas the survivors of Dresden were incidental victims of an act of war and were able to put it behind them.[14] A key difference in the psychology of killing is distance. It's easier to kill when you cannot see your victims.

Freud warned us to "never underestimate the power of the need to obey."[15] In a series of now-famous experiments, Stanley Milgram tested an individual's ability to resist an authority that was not backed up by any external coercive threat. Volunteers were instructed by a "scientific authority" in an alleged learning experiment to inflict an escalating series of fake electric shocks upon a victim, who was actually an actor trained to respond with carefully programmed "voice feedback"—an escalating series of complaints, cries of pain, and calls for help, before

---

13   Martin Gershen. *Destroy or Die: The True Story of My Lai.* New Rochelle, New York: Arlington House, 1971, p. 170.

14   Grossman, pp. 101–105.

15   Grossman, p. 142.

finally putting an end to the experiment. Two-thirds of Milgram's subjects were "obedient" to the point of inflicting extreme pain.[16]

Milgram concluded that under the right circumstances men are led to kill with little difficulty. An evolutionary bias favors the survival of people who can adapt to hierarchical situations and organized social activity. Socialization through family, school, and military service—as well as an array of rewards and punishments within society—reinforce this concept. Notions of loyalty, duty, and discipline become moral imperatives requiring performance in the eyes of authority. Once entangled, people encounter a series of binding factors that make disobedience or refusal even more difficult.[17]

This concept reinforces the notion that leadership on the battlefield is critical in determining whether soldiers will fight and kill. More than a century ago Ardant du Picq noted one incident during the Crimean War in which during heavy fighting, two detachments of soldiers suddenly met unexpectedly face-to-face, at ten paces. They stopped, thunderstruck. Then, forgetting their rifles, they threw stones and withdrew. The reason for this behavior was that neither of the two groups had a decided leader.[18]

The relationship between officer and soldier is unique within the parameters of the need to train soldiers to kill. Certain factors influence the efficacy of training soldiers to kill. It often comes down to proximity of the authority figure to the subject. Another factor is the killer's subjective respect for the authority figure and the intensity of the authority figure's demands for killing behavior. Marshall noted many World War II incidents in which almost all soldiers would fire their

16   Christopher R. Browning. *Ordinary Men: Reserve Police Battalion 101 and the Final Solution in Poland.* New York: HarperCollins, 1992, p. 172.
17   Browning, p. 173.
18   Grossman, p. 144.

weapons while leaders observed them in a combat situation, but when the leaders left, the firing rate immediately dropped to the reported baseline of 15 to 20 percent. To be very effective the killer must bond to their leader, just as he must bond to the group. The leader must also communicate a clear expectation of killing behavior, such as when Lieutenant William L. Calley ordered his men to shoot unarmed civilians at My Lai. He specifically shot many himself to persuade his men to engage in a behavior that they were otherwise reluctant to participate in.[19]

Another mechanism to secure compliance is reinforcing the notion of group absolution. Identification with the group is a powerful motivator; accountability to fellow soldiers is extremely important. In some circumstances the process of group anonymity contributes to killing hysteria, such as was seen in the mass murders that took place in Rwanda in 1994.[20]

The US military is engaged in the process of turning ordinary men into trained and efficient killers. War inevitably entails killing, and those called upon to fight are, more often than not, not the least bit prepared to kill. Military basic training transforms ordinary men into soldiers by utilizing these Milgram factors, which emphasize the demands of authority, group absolution, and distance from the victim, factoring in education, temperament, and life experience.

To increase those firing rates in Vietnam from World War II, the military used a triad of methods: desensitization, conditioning, and denial defense mechanisms. From the very beginning of basic training during Vietnam, killing was the focal point.

"We'd run physical training in the morning and every time your left foot hit the deck you'd have to chant 'kill, kill, kill, kill.' It was

---

19   Grossman, pp. 144–145.
20   Grossman, p. 151.

actually drilled into your mind so much that it seemed like when it actually came down to it, it didn't bother you."—US Marine Corps sergeant and Vietnam War veteran, 1982[21]

The Vietnamese people were dehumanized by the American military. The "mere gook rule," which declared that killing a Vietnamese civilian did not really count, was a common refrain.[22] James Bergthold, a member of Charlie Company and a My Lai veteran, said, "You just couldn't trust nobody in Vietnam and the only good gook was a dead gook."[23]

The Nazis were masters at incorporating dehumanization into military training. The dominant thrust of National Socialist ideology revolved around the two ideas of race and space. Gerhard Weinberg noted that racial vitality and spatial expansion were directly related. In the case of the former, the concept of anti-Semitism, based on a corruption of Social Darwinism and the idea of the survival of the fittest, constituted the central pillar of Hitler's worldview. Hitler blamed the defeat of Germany in World War I on the "Jews and their Marxist fighting organization," which, he claimed, had stabbed the German people in the back. Himmler's SS existed in an organizational environment that created a "new moral order," one in which principles of exclusion and enmity, such as anti-Semitism and anti-Bolshevism, reigned supreme.[24]

Desensitization alone is not enough. The soldier must be conditioned to kill. Vietnam-era basic training included reflexive "quick shoot"

21   Grossman, p. 253.
22   Grossman, p. 190.
23   Gershen, p. 79.
24   Edward B. Westermann. *Hitler's Police Battalions: Enforcing Racial War in the East.* Lawrence, Kansas: University Press of Kansas, 2005, pp. 58 and 234.

exercises. Instead of lying prone on a grassy field shooting at a bull's-eye target, soldiers were trained by standing for hours in full combat equipment in foxholes, looking over an area of terrain. At periodic intervals one or two man-shaped targets would pop up, and each soldier would aim and shoot instantly. The target would fall back like a living target would. This taught soldiers to quickly and accurately engage the targets. By ingraining this shoot-and-kill mentality and giving positive reinforcement for successes, soldiers were gradually conditioned to kill.[25]

The final aspect of the training was the denial defense mechanism: an unconscious method for dealing with the traumatic experience of killing. The soldier would rehearse killing scenarios so many times that when he did kill in combat he was able to, on one level, deny to himself that he was actually killing another human being. This careful rehearsal and realistic mimicry of the act of killing permitted the soldier to convince himself that he had only "engaged" another target. This way an American soldier could convince himself that he was shooting at a silhouette target and not a human being.

The effectiveness of these new training techniques was remarkable. The lopsidedness of combat kill ratios (the number of enemy soldiers killed in comparison to the number of American soldiers killed) in many conflicts since have been substantial: between United States and North Vietnamese during the Vietnam War, British and Argentinean forces during the Falklands War, US and Panamanian forces during the 1989 invasion of Panama, and Coalition forces and insurgents during the war in Iraq. In Vietnam the kill ratio was ten to one—ten North Vietnamese soldiers were killed for every American soldier lost.

One recent example involved US Army Rangers in Somalia. In this incident, made famous by the book and the movie *Black Hawk*

25   Grossman, pp. 255–256.

Down, no artillery or air strikes were used, which makes it an excellent assessment of modern small-arms training techniques. The figures: 18 US troops killed against an estimated 346 Somalis killed.[26] Soldiers felt that they had been "programmed to kill," and in fact they still are. This is one of the reasons the US military remains the most powerful in the world.

---

26   Grossman, pp. 255–258.

CHAPTER 2
Nam

QUANG Ngai province sits in the north of what was once South Vietnam. Nam Viets, refugees who fled from China to escape the harsh rule there, settled just south of Danang in Quang Ngai about twenty-five hundred years ago. This area, constituting a bulge in the Southeast Asian peninsula along the coast of South China Sea, was perfect in many ways. The sea was filled with fish, easily caught. The lowlands, drained and washed by the Cho Mai and the other rivers to the north, by the Tra Khuc to the south, and by myriad streams in between, were ideal for growing rice and vegetables and for grazing buffalo. Also, except for the rainy season and the floods of late fall and early winter—which were almost necessary, anyway, if the rice were to grow—the weather was always warm and pleasant.[27]

Eventually four villages, called My Lai, Co Luy, My Khe, and Tu Cung, sprang up and dominated Quang Ngai province. They would later become one village called Son My, with My Lai along the coast to the northeast. The villages of Son My were embedded in the earth

27   Richard Hammer. *One Morning in the War: The Tragedy at Son My.* New York: Coward-McCann, 1970, pp. 24–25.

and part of the fabric of the land. The people settled down, fished and farmed, raised their families, and in good times, prospered.[28]

The Vietnamese prided themselves less on their conquests than on their ability to resist and to survive. Living under the great wing of China, they bought their independence and maintained it only at a high price of blood. Throughout their history they have had to acknowledge the preponderance of the great Middle Kingdom both as the power and as the hub of culture. The Vietnamese knew their place in the world and guarded it jealously.[29]

The Vietnamese worshipped their ancestors as the source of their lives, their fortunes, and their civilization. In the rites of ancestor worship, the child imitated the gestures of the grandfather, so when he became the grandfather he could repeat them exactly to his grandchildren. Death marked no final end. Buried in the rice fields that sustained his family, the father would live on in the bodies of his children and grandchildren. In this continuum of the family, private property did not exist, for the father was a trustee of the land to be passed on to his children. To the Vietnamese the land itself was the sacred, constant element. For the traditional villager, who spent his life immobile, bound to the rice land of his predecessors, the world was indeed a very small place.[30]

The French arrived in the nineteenth century, posing a challenge to the Vietnamese social order and changing the country permanently. The Vietnamese were faced with the enormous challenge of preserving their traditional way of life while living under colonial rule and assimilating the French culture. The French colonials pretty much left the Vietnamese alone, particularly in the villages.

---

28 Hammer, p. 27.
29 Frances Fitzgerald. *Fire In The Lake: The Vietnamese and the Americans in Vietnam.* Boston: Little, Brown and Company, 1972, p. 8.
30 Fitzgerald, pp. 9–10.

For the most part the Vietnamese resisted efforts from the outside to encroach and bring change. But change did come in the form of the Japanese in World War II. The Japanese drove out the French, which inspired a new resistance movement among Vietnamese nationals. Most young men joined the Viet Minh and other resistance movements that were fighting the Japanese. After the war the French did not immediately return, but Quang Ngai had become a center of Viet Minh strength. This was the case both in 1945, when the Viet Minh proclaimed itself the government of the nation of Vietnam, and later, when war between the French and the Viet Minh broke out.

One of the major Viet Minh leaders, Pham Van Dong, later to become prime minister of North Vietnam, was born and raised in Quang Ngai, south of the four villages. In the province, Pham Van Dong and Ho Chi Minh were both hailed as heroes and patriots.[31]

After the 1954 partition of the country some semblance of normalcy returned to Quang Ngai. The province still harbored a strong connection to the north, and many from Son My traveled north after the partitioning to make a new life under the government they had fought for. Soon thereafter the administration of President Ngo Dinh Diem began collecting taxes and engaging in land redistribution reforms that did not sit well with many in Quang Ngai. The tax collectors were more corrupt than those under the Viet Minh, and it did not take long for the residents of Quang Ngai to become disenchanted with the Diem regime. Mostly Buddhists, the people heard of the ongoing abuse of Buddhists by Diem operatives and felt deep resentment and growing bitterness. The Diem regime had planted the seeds of revolt in Quang Ngai, and those seeds grew rapidly. The Viet Minh was reborn as the Viet Cong in the mountains of Quang Ngai in 1959.[32]

---

31   Hammer, p. 29.
32   Hammer, pp. 37–38.

In spite of the political turmoil, for the most part the peasants had little interest in politics. The Vietnamese had seen many rulers, and over the years little had really changed. In their experience the Vietnamese had come to believe there was only a difference of degree, not of kind, between almost all who had ruled them. The people of Quang Ngai and many other villages all over Vietnam tried to remain aloof from the struggle erupting around them. No matter who was in control, they were convinced their lives would remain basically as they always had.[33]

All that changed in the winter of 1963 and 1964. Some of the men who had gone north ten years before returned to Quang Ngai with a message: The VC were taking control of the village of Son My, and they had weapons to enforce the message if anyone resisted. The conquest wasn't hard, as they had support from relatives they had left behind. With that the VC effectively sealed the area from the outside so no one with any power within the South Vietnamese government could dispute them.

Though, it was made clear that the village would not be totally isolated. The people could go to market as they always had, and some officials from the government might come to the village on occasion. But it was made known to all that this territory was under VC control.[34]

The VC tried to generate support for their cause, but they found a populace with little enthusiasm for ideology. They collected war taxes but did not abuse any of the people. Those VC members in positions of control in Son My were natives of the village. They knew there was little chance of winning the unqualified support of most of the peasants. It was just not the way of the people. Yet the VC wanted control of Son My for the shelter and manpower it provided. If it was prosperous, the

---

33   Hammer, p. 40.
34   Hammer, p. 47.

taxes assessed in rice could be used to feed large numbers of VC and, later, North Vietnamese Army regulars in the field.

However, the arrival of the VC brought attention from the government, and it was not long before Son My became contested. Army of the Republic of Vietnam (ARVN) troops moved in and drove out the VC. A few days later the VC struck back, taking control of the territory once again. Each skirmish drove more people from Son My.

Once American forces arrived in large numbers, Son My saw still more action. On three separate occasions in late 1967 and early 1968, American patrols appeared in Xom Lang. Nguyen To, a sixty-four-year-old native, said, "Three times the GIs operate in my hamlet. They stay all day and talk with people, especially the children who swarmed around them and would say, 'Okay! Okay! Okay! Hello! Hello! Hello!' And the GIs would give them canned fruits and candy. And the people gave them rice and asked the GIs into their homes. At the time the GIs were very friendly to them." Asked if any shots were fired at the GIs, To said, "No, no shots."[35]

For the people of Son My in Quang Ngai province things were settling down. They seemed to get along with the VC without much friction, and the Americans had been friendly when they had come. The government had assured them the area was safe, and there had been no leaflets or warnings that they were in any danger.[36] Life was back to normal.

---

35 Hammer, pp. 57–58.
36 Hammer, p. 60.

Chapter 3
Charlie Company

"The best company in Hawaii."

That is what Lieutenant William L. Calley called the unit he joined upon reporting to the Eleventh Light Brigade at Schofield Barracks. It was Company C, First Battalion, Twentieth Infantry, also known as Charlie Company because *C* is *Charlie* in the phonetic alphabet used in military communications.[37] Lieutenant Colonel Frank A. Barker commanded Charlie Company. The commanding officer of the Eleventh Brigade was Colonel Oran K. Henderson. The division commander was Major General Samuel W. Koster. All three men were career military officers—also called "lifers"—with plentiful military experience.

The 150 men who made up Charlie Company were fairly typical of the American combat soldiers in Vietnam. Educationally, 87 percent were high school graduates. In other areas—general intelligence, trainability, and aptitude—Charlie Company also differed little from

---

37   Michal R. Belknap. *The Vietnam War on Trial: The My Lai Massacre and the Court-Martial of Lieutenant Calley.* Lawrence, Kansas: University Press of Kansas, 2002, p. 37.

the Army as a whole. Only thirteen of the soldiers came from what came to be called McNamara's 100,000, the project of 100,000 men well below the Army average in terms of aptitude and intelligence and deemed unlikely to meet peacetime entry qualifications. Most of the men were between eighteen and twenty-two years of age, and nearly half were black.[38] Most were reluctant draftees whose role was to replace soldiers killed in combat. The company was poorly motivated, but that was not atypical of a combat unit in Vietnam.

The military had established a one-year-only policy for Army combat troops, meaning no one was to remain in Vietnam for longer than one year. By the time a soldier had garnered sufficient experience to fight a guerrilla war, he was ready to go home. Even more importantly, having only one year in a war zone made a soldier more cautious in combat.[39] This constant troop rotation also undermined unit morale and cohesiveness.

Most of the troops sent to Vietnam lacked the educational deferments or political connections to avoid service in Vietnam. For many this was the first time they had been away from home. They were shipped to a strange country where the people and customs were totally alien to them. They were dropped into a war that had no clear objective. Their enemy was invisible, yet he was all around them. The enemy was the very ground they walked on; the ground was deadly, littered with land mines or booby traps that could kill or maim. Eventually every soldier would become filled with fear and hate. Soon everyone would become the enemy, the object of that fear and hate, for if you trusted no one and hated everyone, maybe you would survive.[40]

Charlie Company's commander was a man named Captain Ernest

38   Michael Bilton and Kevin Sim. *Four Hours in My Lai*. New York: Viking, 1971, pp. 50–51.
39   Gershen, pp. 57–58.
40   Hammer, pp. 64–65.

Medina. A Mexican-American and a career military officer, Medina was ambitious, looking to get a promotion to major. He knew that with his limited education the only way to get a promotion was to get combat experience. He wanted to go to Vietnam. So when Medina took over Charlie Company he worked them very hard. Tough but fair, Medina was generally well regarded by the men under his command.

Three lieutenants served under Medina: William L. Calley, Jeffrey LaCrosse, and Stephen Brooks. Calley was the least respected and was loathed by most of the men in his platoon. His premilitary life was not distinguished. Growing up in Miami, Florida, he was a poor student, small in stature (five-foot-four) and generally nondescript. He flunked out of junior college, drifted from job to job, and traveled cross-country, looking for meaningful employment. In 1966, while in San Francisco, his mail caught up with him, and he received a draft notice.

On his way back to Miami his car broke down in Albuquerque, New Mexico, so he went to the nearest recruiting station to request advice on how best to respond to his draft notice and was advised to enlist.[41] Because he had attended a military prep school for one year in high school, Calley was admitted into Officer Candidate School. Junior officers were suffering a very high rate of casualty in Vietnam, so the standards for admission to OCS were lowered to meet the need for more bodies.

In Vietnam, Calley's men were very aware of his limitations. He was constantly trying to impress Medina, but most of the men felt Medina had little regard for Calley. Calley admitted he was "an inadequate leader"; for instance, he could not read a map or a compass. His men wondered how he ever got through OCS.[42]

Charlie Company arrived in Vietnam in December 1967 and was

---

41   Bilton and Sim, p. 50.
42   Belknap, pp. 35 and 39.

sent to Quang Ngai Province in the central highlands. The general plan was for Charlie Company to engage and destroy the Forty-Eighth Local Force Battalion of the Viet Cong. Quang Ngai was a VC stronghold, and US intelligence was convinced the Forty-Eighth was in Quang Ngai and was vulnerable.

Unfortunately, the Tet Offensive in January 1968 dispelled any notion that the Viet Cong were demoralized or defeated. Search-and-destroy missions were fruitless, and morale became a problem; the troops were chasing phantoms. There was nothing to show for the long, hot, exhausting days tramping through paddy fields and friendless villages.[43]

By mid-February Charlie Company began to take casualties. Booby traps, snipers, and the occasional ambush began to take their toll on company morale. Additionally, Calley proved to an ineffective leader. His poor judgment often exposed his men to enemy fire, which inflicted many casualties. But Calley had learned the protocol of body count culture early.[44] Sadly, the standard by which the military leadership measured success was by the number of dead enemy soldiers. Body counts were routinely demanded of junior officers, which inevitably led to higher rates of civilian casualties. Calley attempted to mask his incompetence by providing exaggerated reports of body counts.

As the month went on Charlie Company was beginning to crack under the pressure. Michael Bernhardt, a member of Calley's platoon, recalled an incident whereby the platoon spotted a woman and a child on the far side of a field. While taking a break, several soldiers walked across the field, grabbed the woman, and threw her to the ground. Then one by one they raped her while the child stood by, screaming, wriggling in the grasp of one of the soldiers. When they were finished,

---

43   Bilton and Sim, pp. 67 and 70.
44   Bilton and Sim, pp. 71–72.

one of the men took his rifle and casually shot the woman through the head. He turned and just as casually killed the child.[45]

As these sorts of incidents mounted the Americans began to see the Vietnamese people as some subhuman species. To kill them became no more a crime than to spray DDT on an annoying insect. The value of human life, of Vietnamese civilian life, diminished more and more. Fear and hatred of the Vietnamese grew stronger in the Americans every day, though these feelings were depersonalized.[46]

Charlie Company continued to suffer casualties while never actually engaging in a direct confrontation with the enemy. This only added to their frustration. Varnado Simpson, a member of Calley's platoon, lamented, "Who is the enemy? How can you distinguish between the civilians and the noncivilians? The same people who come and work in the bases at daytime, they just want to shoot and kill you at nighttime. How do you distinguish between the good and the bad? All of them look the same."[47]

Things took a turn for the worse when the company, while on patrol, walked into an innocuous-seeming field on February 25, 1968. The field, laced with mines and booby traps, began to explode in quick order as the men began to scream and run in panic. The air echoed with screams, and blood and human flesh and bones flew everywhere. The carnage was horrible; one soldier described a scene of a human body being cut open from neck to crotch: "[One soldier] was cleaved down the middle ... The chest cavity was open. I could see the intestines and the stomach, and his lungs were moving."[48]

---

45   Hammer, p. 104.

46   Hammer, p. 105.

47   James S. Olson and Randy Roberts. *My Lai: A Brief History with Documents.* New York: Bedford Books, 1998, p. 16.

48   Gershen, p. 246.

The company suffered six fatalities and twelve wounded.[49] They were mad and anxious to avenge the deaths of their comrades. Three weeks later they were told by Captain Medina the opportunity for revenge was imminent, as they were about to conduct a combat assault on a village known as My Lai, where intelligence had discovered that the Viet Cong Forty-Eighth Battalion was now located.[50]

---

49   Hammer, p. 106.
50   Belknap, p. 57.

CHAPTER 4
My Lai

THE information of the whereabouts of the Forty-Eighth Battalion was based upon Army intelligence and local informants. Reports indicated that the Viet Cong had been making a base in Son My village in the hamlet of My Lai. As the Americans were often confused by Vietnamese terminology, it is not surprising that this information was misunderstood. American military maps showed more than one My Lai. There were six of them. Where the Viet Cong were, My Khe, was the sub-hamlet the Americans called My Lai, and on their maps it was shaded in pink. The Americans called it Pinkville.[51]

The plan was for a direct attack that would destroy the Viet Cong battalion as well as the village and all other hamlets supporting the Viet Cong. The night before the assault, Captain Medina told the men of Charlie Company that they would be going to battle and that all the civilians would be gone to market by the time the company landed.[52] "Medina told them we had permission, Lieutenant Colonel Barker had received permission from the ARVNs, that the village could be

---

51   Hammer, pp. 108–109.
52   Gershen, p. 286.

destroyed since it was a VC stronghold, to burn the houses down, to kill all the livestock, to cut any of the crops that might feed the VC, to cave the wells, and destroy the village."[53]

Somebody at the briefing asked him: do we kill women and children? It was an unusual question, but herein lies the quandary, as the testimony is disputed. Medina testified that his answer was, "No, you do not kill women and children. You use common sense. If they have a weapon and try to engage you, then you can shoot back."[54]

But many of the men took away a different message. Sergeant Kenneth Hodges recalled: "This was a time for us to get even ... The order we were given was to kill and destroy everything that was in the village. It was to kill the pigs, drop them in wells; pollute the water supply, kill, cut down the banana trees, burn the village; burn the hootches ... It was clearly explained that there were to be no prisoners."

Staff Sergeant Bacon: "We were to kill all the Viet Cong and Viet Cong sympathizers in the village."

Staff Sergeant Martin Fagan said "Kill everyone."

Medina said: "Kill everything that moves."[55]

Others disputed that explicit orders were given to kill civilians. "It was like Medina's benediction," Michael Bernhardt said. "He didn't actually say to kill every man, woman, and child in My Lai. He stopped just short of saying that. He gave every indication that that's what he expected."[56]

The Peers Report, the report of the official Army investigation of the My Lai massacre, confirmed the testimony of those who said Medina had ordered the destruction of the village. It is less clear on the issue

53   Bilton and Sim, p. 98.
54   Bilton and Sim, p. 98.
55   Bilton and Sim, p. 99.
56   Bilton and Sim, p. 101.

of killing civilians. Some of the testimony heard by the Commission is as follows:

"When we left the briefing we felt we were going to have a lot of resistance and we knew we were supposed to kill everyone in the village."—William Calvin Lloyd, First Platoon, C/1-20 Infantry

"That evening, as we cleaned our weapons and got our gear ready, we talked about the operation. People were talking about killing everything that moved. Everyone knew what we were going to do." —Robert Wayne Pendleton, Third Platoon, C/1-20 Infantry

"We were all psyched up because we wanted revenge for some of our fallen comrades that had been killed prior to this operation in the general area of Pinkville."—Allen Joseph Boyce, First Platoon, C/1-20 Infantry

"It seemed like it was a chance to get revenge or something like that for the lives we had lost."—Tommy L. Moss, Second Platoon, C/1-20 Infantry[57]

At dawn the following morning, March 16, 1968, eight UH-1-E troop-carrying helicopters arrived at Landing Zone Dottie and began to ferry the men of Charlie Company to battle. Arriving at their destination, the troops disembarked from the choppers and spread out in the elephant grass to make their way toward the target. They were anticipating a "hot" landing zone, meaning they were expecting enemy

---

57   Joseph Goldstein, Burke Marshall, and Jack Schwartz. *The My Lai Massacre and Its Cover-Up: Beyond the Reach of Law? The Peers Commission Report.* New York: The Free Press, 1976, pp. 99–100.

fire immediately, but instead it was remarkably quiet. Medina noted the lack of armed resistance. Although a helicopter pilot reported small arms fire, it was most likely from American soldiers firing their weapons on their way to the village.[58]

As they approached the first houses, the soldiers broke into smaller squads. What precipitated the slaughter is unclear. Private Paul Meadlo, a member of Calley's platoon, stated: "There was one man, a gook in a shelter, all huddled down in there, and the soldier called out and said there's a gook over here. Sergeant Mitchell gave orders to shoot. And so the man was shot and we moved into the village."[59]

"We went in shooting," Charles West remembered. "We'd shoot into the hootches and there were people running around. There were big craters in the village from the preattack bombing. I saw some of the people, some were women and kids all torn up." The contagion of slaughter was spreading throughout the platoon.[60]

James Bergthold came across a hut that had been raked with bullets. Inside he found three children, a woman with a flesh wound to her side, and an old man squatting down, hardly able to move. Bergthold shot him in the head with his pistol, claiming it was an act of mercy. Harry Stanley observed that the fleeing villagers offered no resistance. His friend Alan Boyce grabbed a farmer; Boyce pushed the man toward Stanley and then stabbed him with his bayonet for no reason. Boyce then grabbed another man, shot him in the neck, and dropped him down a well, lobbing an M-26 grenade in after him. "That's the way you gotta do it," he told Simpson.[61]

Dennis Conti stated that the shooting, once it began, created almost a chain reaction. Families had huddled together for safety in houses,

58   Hammer, p. 119.
59   Hammer, p. 121.
60   Hammer, p. 121.
61   Bilton and Sim, p. 112.

in the yards, and in bunkers, only to be mown down with automatic weapons fire or blown apart by fragmentation grenades. Women and children were thrown and pushed into bunkers and grenades thrown in after them. At one point, wandering off on his own, Conti found a woman aged about twenty with a four-year-old child. He forced her to perform oral sex on him while he held a gun at the child's head, threatening to kill the child. Lieutenant Calley ordered Conti to stop and get back into formation.[62]

In the northern part of the village the carnage continued. Children aged only six or seven came toward the soldiers with their hands outstretched, saying, "Chop, chop." They were asking for the food and candy they had received from other American soldiers on previous visits to the village. The soldiers gunned them down.

The villagers had huddled together for safety, but the Americans poured gunfire into them, tearing their bodies apart. One man fired a machine gun at random, others using their M-16s on automatic.

Some soldiers refused to take part in the slaughter. Dennis Bunning informed his squad leader, Sergeant Hodges, he would not take part in killing women and children. He was ordered to the far left flank, away from the civilians.

Deeper into the village the First Platoon had collected a large group of about sixty Vietnamese. They were made to squat down. Calley appeared with his radio operator, Charles Sledge. Calley ordered them to "take care of them." After the men failed to respond to Calley's order, he said, "I thought I told you to take care of them."

Meadlo responded, "We are. We are watching over them."

Calley's response was, "I want them killed." Losing his temper, Calley called Meadlo into line and told him, "Fire when I say fire."[63]

62   Bilton and Sim, p. 113.
63   Bilton and Sim, p. 120.

Standing side by side only ten feet from their victims, Calley and Meadlo blazed away, changing magazines from time to time. The Vietnamese screamed, yelled, and tried to get up. It was pure carnage as heads were shot off along with limbs; the fleshier body parts were ripped to shreds. The victims were mostly women and children, babies to early teens in age. After a few minutes Conti could see a few children left standing, as mothers had thrown themselves on top of the young ones to protect them from the hail of bullets. The children were trying to stand up. Calley opened fire again, killing them one by one.

The soldiers pushed ahead to the far end of the village. Calley instructed them, "We have another job to do." Another forty to fifty Vietnamese were being held by some soldiers near an irrigation ditch. Other members of the First Platoon brought more Vietnamese to the ditch. Calley told machine gunner Robert Maples, "Load your machine gun and shoot these people."

Maples declined the order. Calley pointed his weapon at Maples, others stepped in to protect Maples, and Calley backed off. Then Calley and Meadlo began firing into the ditch. The Vietnamese tried frantically to hide under one another, mothers protecting babies. The soldiers watching saw remnants of human beings, hundreds of pieces of flesh and bone, flying up in the air as the shallow ravine was repeatedly sprayed with bullets. Magazine after magazine was reloaded during the mass execution.

The sadistic behavior was not limited to mass killings. Several soldiers became "double veterans," GI slang for raping a woman and then murdering her. Many women were raped, sodomized, and mutilated, including having their vaginas ripped open with knives or bayonets. Soldiers repeatedly stabbed their victims, cut off limbs, sometimes beheaded them. In My Lai, Varnado Simpson watched three men go into a hooch with a girl aged about seventeen, where she was held down and raped. When they were finished they shot her dead, her face completely blown away. About half a kilometer to the north, outside of a hooch, Private Gonzalez encountered a pile of seven naked women aged between eighteen and thirty-five, their corpses dotted all over with tiny, dark holes. They had resisted sexual assault and were killed with several buckshot rounds fired at close range from an M-79 grenade launcher.

Medina was on the outskirts of My Lai and was aware something bad was going on from the lack of radio chatter, which would be expected when a battle was under way, but he did not realize the magnitude of it until he saw it with his own eyes. Medina himself shot a woman under dubious circumstances. He had radioed immediately after the shooting stopped to Lieutenant Colonel Barker that only twenty-eight civilians had been killed, although he knew that was a lie. There had been no firefight, and not a single shot had been fired at his men.

Were it not for the bravery of Lieutenant Hugh Thompson, a helicopter pilot who flew reconnaissance missions as part of the 123rd Aviation Battalion, the massacre would have claimed even more lives. Thompson flew an H-23 helicopter, a craft known as a "bubble ship" because of the bubble-shaped cockpit that gave the crew an all-around view of the ground. Flying around My Lai the morning of March 16, 1968, Thompson saw wounded civilians, who he marked for pickup. He then witnessed an infantry officer shoot a woman at close range. Shortly thereafter he saw the dozens of civilian bodies in the irrigation ditch, some of which were moving.

He immediately landed his helicopter and confronted Lieutenant Calley. Calley told Thompson that he was in charge of the operation. Thompson lifted off and immediately saw the shooting resume near the ditch. He immediately radioed for help from nearby helicopter gunships and then landed, placing his helicopter between Calley's men and the civilian detainees and ordering his gunners to point their weapons at the American soldiers. His instructions were to shoot the American soldiers if they tried to kill civilians.

The backup gunships arrived and evacuated the remaining Vietnamese. Charlie Company was ordered to cease fire. The men took a lunch break. The killing had stopped.[64]

---

64   Bilton and Sim, pp. 111–141.

CHAPTER 5
Cover~up

CHARLIE Company had killed over four hundred innocent Vietnamese civilians at My Lai. Most were women and children. Hugh Thompson reported what he had witnessed to his superiors. It was hard to keep this matter a secret, although it appears some in the Army tried.

Thompson's first report was to his commanding officer, Major Frederick Watke. Watke passed this on to his superior, Lieutenant Colonel John L. Holladay. Watke and Holladay met with Brigadier General George H. Young. Young then informed Major General Samuel Koster. Meanwhile Medina had instructed the members of Charlie Company to refrain from discussing the incident with anyone.

On Monday, March 18, 1968, Young and Colonel Oran Henderson met with Lieutenant Colonel Barker as well as Watke and Holladay. Instead of notifying the inspector general, they assigned lower-ranking officers to speak with Warrant Officer Hugh Thompson. Colonel Henderson then met with Captain Medina, who advised him that Charlie Company had not intentionally caused any civilian deaths.[65] A brief and perfunctory investigation took place that concluded no violation of the military code of engagement had occurred.[66]

Interestingly, all of this took place even though the Army knew an Army photographer had accompanied Charlie Company into My Lai and had taken photos of the massacre. Sergeant Ronald Haeberle's photographs would later become famous. He was in My Lai and had failed to interfere with the massacre, taking the position that as a photographer, his professional obligation was to observe and photograph and not interfere. He was later censured by the report of the Peers Commission.[67]

The official Combat Action Report for the attack on My Lai reported 128 enemy troops killed, two US soldiers killed, and the recovery of three rifles and assorted ammunition. Lieutenant Colonel Frank A. Barker submitted this report on March 28, 1968,[68] making him a key player in the cover-up. Charlie Company continued with its search-and-destroy missions until its year's time in Vietnam was up, and Barker was killed in a helicopter crash in June 1968.

The South Vietnamese knew of the incident, and it was a boon to the efforts of the Viet Cong to secure public support for their cause. It took twenty months for the American public to learn of the events at My Lai. By early 1969 many in Charlie Company had left the Army, while others had transferred to other units. But a former GI, Ron Ridenhour, had heard stories from other soldiers of the massacre

---

65   Belknap, pp. 82–84.

66   Olson and Roberts, p. 24.

67   Belknap, p. 91.

68   Olson and Roberts, pp. 28–29.

at Pinkville, and he wrote a letter in 1969 to several Congressmen, requesting an investigation.

Numerous investigations ensued, including one by the Army under the leadership of Lieutenant General William R. Peers. Peers conducted a thorough investigation of the massacre and the cover-up. His report was made public on March 14, 1970.

Peers made a series of findings, and based on these he set forth several recommendations. The Commission's first finding was that on March 16, 1968, troops of Task Force Barker massacred a large number of Vietnamese civilians in the village of Son My. The Commission further concluded that knowledge of the incident had existed at the company level and at the Eleventh Brigade command level. The subsequent efforts at concealment had resulted in suppression of a war crime of great magnitude. The concealment was deliberate, prior investigations had been superficial and misleading, and efforts had been made at every level to suppress information. The Commission recommended court-martial or disciplinary action against thirty officers.[69]

---

69   Goldstein, Marshall, and Schwartz, pp. 55–56 and 320–345.

CHAPTER 6
The Calley Trial

EVERY soldier in Vietnam was issued a pocket card that contained nine rules for dealing with Vietnamese civilians. The cards were from the MACV (Military Assistance Command Vietnam). A copy is contained in Appendix A. Among the rules were, "Treat women with politeness and respect," and, "Above all else you are members of the US Military Forces on a difficult mission, responsible for all your official and personal actions. Reflect honor upon yourself and the United States of America."

All United States military personnel are subject to and bound by the Geneva Convention, a treaty the United States entered into with other nations in August 1949. The Geneva Convention established standards of treatment for noncombatants in a war zone. Article 3 of the Geneva Convention "prohibits at any time and in any place whatsoever violence to life and person, in particular murder of all kinds, mutilation, cruel treatment and torture against persons taking no active part in combat, who have laid down their arms or placed in detention."[70]

The United States Army Field Manual in effect in 1968 specifically incorporated the provisions of the Geneva Convention and forbade the killing of prisoners. Individual soldiers were to be held accountable for criminal conduct, and in some cases military commanders would be responsible for the war crimes committed by their subordinate members of the armed forces or by other persons subject to their control.[71] Additionally, Article 118 of the Uniform Code of Military Justice subjects a soldier to the charge of murder "if he or she has a premeditated design to kill, intends to kill or inflict great bodily harm or is engaged in an act which is inherently dangerous to others and evinces a wanton disregard of human life or is engaged in burglary, rape, sodomy, robbery or aggravated arson."[72]

Wilson's investigation had taken him all over the country, interviewing former members of Charlie Company and collecting statements and evidence. Calley himself refused to be interviewed. He was returned to Fort Benning, Georgia, in June 1969 and given an administrative assignment.

The military retains jurisdiction over military personnel only for as long as they are in military service. Many of the participants at My Lai had left the service by the time the Peers Commission had wrapped up its report.

On September 5, 1969, one day before he expected to be discharged from the Army, First Lieutenant William Laws Calley was charged with four specifications of murder under Article 118 of the Military Code of Justice, alleging the murder of not fewer than 104 civilians at My Lai on

---

70   Goldstein, Marshall, Schwartz, p. 444.
71   Goldstein, Marshall, Schwartz, pp. 455–456.
72   Uniform Code of Military Justice, Article 118. www.au.af.mil/au/awc /awcgate/ucmj.

March 16, 1968.[73] This set the stage for the most famous court-martial in American history.

At first the charges received little attention. However, after the brilliant reporting of journalist Seymour Hersh, who broke the story on November 13, 1969, and the publication of the Peers Report in March 1970, the media quickly made the Calley court-martial a lightning rod for both proponents and opponents of the war. War hawks not only tried to minimize the massacre but also attempted to question if it even happened. Public opinion revealed a substantial amount of skepticism among the American public. Americans seemed inclined to assign responsibility for whatever had happened to the war itself rather than to the men of Charlie Company. The war was becoming increasingly unpopular. Calley actually received a great deal of sympathy for he was, to many, a scapegoat for a failed war effort.[74]

The Nixon administration saw the Calley case as a distraction and an attempt by antiwar forces to undermine support for the war effort. Nixon supporters on Capitol Hill began to discredit Calley's critics, such as Ridenhour and Hugh Thompson. Congress commenced investigations in the hope of finding no wrongdoing before the court-martial began.

The court-martial was convened on November 17, 1970. Captain Aubrey Daniel led the prosecution, assisted by Captain John Patrick Partin. George Latimer, a civilian attorney who "had a towering reputation in military law,"[75] represented Calley. He had sat on the United States Court of Military Appeals, the nation's highest military court. Calley's military defense counsel was Major Kenneth Albert Raby, a career Judge Advocate General officer well regarded in military

---

73   Bilton and Sim, pp. 246–247.
74   Belknap, pp. 130–131.
75   Belknap, pp. 130–131.

legal circles. The presiding judge was Colonel Reid W. Kennedy. The jury was comprised of six military officers, all of whom were combat veterans and five of whom had seen action in Vietnam. All jurors claimed to have little knowledge of the My Lai incident.

Captain Daniel presented a forceful argument for conviction. He set forth all of the allegations and explained to the jury how he would provide eyewitness testimony of the murders Calley was accused of perpetrating. Interestingly, although Daniel could not identify any of the victims by name, he was able to describe them with sufficient detail to confirm they were Vietnamese civilians.

Daniel began his case by calling eyewitnesses who could establish that Charley Company had encountered no resistance at My Lai that day. Frank Beardslee, a rifleman, testified that Charley Company had received no hostile fire during the operation. He had even declined a Combat Infantryman's Badge offered by Lieutenant Colonel Barker because he knew there had been no "combat."

Photographer Ronald Haeberle testified to having seen homes and crops destroyed and having witnessed the massacre of a group of civilians. He had also photographed a pile of murdered Vietnamese.[76]

Dennis Conti told the court that "they [a group of civilians] were pretty well messed up. There was a lot of heads had been shot off, pieces of heads, flesh of the … fleshy parts of the body, side and arms pretty well messed up. I seen the recoil of the rifle and the muzzle flashes and as I looked down, I seen a woman try to get up. As she got up I saw Lt. Calley fire and hit the side of her head and blow the side of her head off. I left."[77]

Paul Meadlo also testified for the prosecution. His testimony was

---

76 Belknap, pp. 157–158.
77 Bilton and Sim, pp. 334–335.

very compelling. What follows are his statements under the direct examination of Aubrey Daniel:

Q. How many people did you gather up in the village?
A. Between thirty and fifty.

Q. Did you see Lt. Calley?
A. Yes.

Q. What did he do?
A. He came up to me and he said, "You know what to do with them, Meadlo." I assumed he wanted me to guard them.

Q. What were the people doing there?
A. They were just standing there. Calley said, "How come they're not dead?" I said I didn't know we were supposed to kill them. He said, "I want them dead." He backed off twenty or thirty feet and started shooting into the people—the Viet Cong—shooting automatic. He was beside me. He burned four or five magazines. I burned off a few, about three. I helped shoot 'em.

Q. Were there any other Vietnamese there?
A. Yes, there was Viet Cong there. About seventy-five to a hundred. Then Lt. Calley called to me and said, "We've got another job to do, Meadlo."

Q. What happened then?
A. He started shoving them off and shooting them in the ravine.

Q. How many times did he shoot?
A. I can't remember.

Q. Did you shoot?
A. Yes, I shot the Viet Cong, he ordered me to help kill people. I
   started shoving them off and shooting.

Q. How long did you fire?
A. I don't know.

Q. Did you change magazines?
A. Yes.

Q. Did Calley change magazines?
A. Yes.

Q. How many times did he change magazines?
A. Ten to fifteen times.

Q. How many bullets in a magazine?
A. Twenty, normally.

Daniels also called Hugh Thompson to testify, who described what
he had seen as he was flying over My Lai on March 16. "There was just
a lot of bodies in there sir—women, kids, babies and old men."[78]

Thomas Turner, another member of Charlie Company, testified
that as he approached the drainage ditch he saw Meadlo and other
GIs firing into it. Calley had emptied his weapon, changed clips, and
started shooting again. Turner sat on a dike just north of the ditch for

78   Belknap, p. 160.

over an hour, watching as small groups of people were herded into it and as Calley systematically executed them. He also said he had seen his platoon leader shoot a young Vietnamese woman who was coming toward him with her hands up.[79]

Calley's defense was that he was merely following orders. On direct examination by his attorney, George Latimer:

Q. Did you receive training, which had to do with the obedience to orders?

A. Yes, that all orders were to be assumed legal, that the soldier's job was to carry out any order given to him to the best of his ability.

Q. What might occur if you disobeyed an order by a senior officer?

A. You could be court-martialed for refusing an order and refusing an order in the face of the enemy. You could be sent to death, sir.

Q. Were you required to make a determination of the legality of an order?

A. No sir, I was never told I had the choice, sir.

On the incident at the irrigation ditch:

Q. There has been testimony that you stood at the ditch for a considerable time and fired for an hour and a half as the groups were marched up. Did you do that?

A. No sir, I did not.

Q. Why did you give Meadlo the order that if he could not get rid of them to waste them?

---

79   Belknap, pp. 162–163.

A. Because that was my order. That was the order of the day.

Q. Who gave you that order?
A. My commanding officer, Captain Medina.

Upon further examination, Calley testified, "Well, I was ordered to go in there and destroy the enemy. That was my job on that day. That was the mission I was given. I did not sit down and think in terms of men, women, and children. They were all classified the same, and that classification that we dealt with, just as enemy soldiers."[80]

By most accounts the Calley defense was weak and disorganized. Latimer tried to discredit the prosecution's witnesses upon cross-examination but to little avail. The defense then tried to establish Calley's lack of intent to commit murder by introducing a report by two medical "experts" who testified that Calley had suffered from impairments of both volition and cognition and had acted like a robot, knowing but not understanding what he was doing. This diminished capacity defense fell flat as Dr. Albert A. LaVerne, the defense's psychiatrist, admitted his conclusions were not based on any interviews he had had with Calley.

Calley admitted to ordering Meadlo to "waste" some prisoners if he could not move them, though he said he had done so only once. He denied issuing the directive and insisted the order to kill them had originated with Captain Medina. He further acknowledged receiving neither enemy fire nor any information that his men had suffered any casualties. He claimed everyone in the village "was the enemy" and needed to be destroyed.

For the prosecution, Captain Daniels refuted the psychiatric testimony by calling three psychiatrists from Walter Reed Army Medical

---

80   Trial transcripts of the court-martial of William Calley, p. 6.

Center who had conducted the sanity board exam of Calley and found him to be sane. He then called Captain Medina to the stand.

Medina recounted the briefing of March 15, 1968. He testified that in response to a question he told his men that "they were not to kill women and children." He denied ordering Calley to kill or "waste" any Vietnamese person. He denied Calley's report of having told him the people were slowing him down.

After, Medina survived a lengthy cross-examination. However, he admitted to killing one woman because he thought she had a hand grenade. He also acknowledged his role in the cover-up, claiming he feared the incident would embarrass the Army.[81]

The case concluded with closing arguments and went to the jury. After ten days of deliberation, Calley was found guilty of murdering twenty-two civilians as well as assault with intent to commit murder. The day after rendering the verdict the jury sentenced him to be confined to hard labor for life and to forfeit all pay and allowances.

In August 1971 Captain Medina was charged with the murder of 102 Vietnamese civilians. At the heart of the case against Medina was the concept of command responsibility. The question at hand was, as the commander of Charlie Company, should Medina be held accountable for the actions of his men at My Lai? The government believed that Medina knew what was happening in the village and failed to stop it.

In its brief to the Court, the prosecution asserted, "In general, a commander is responsible for the actions of his subordinates in the performance of their duties. The responsibility of a commander for controlling and supervising his subordinates is the cornerstone of a responsible armed force. A commander must give clear, concise orders and must be sure they are understood. After taking action or issuing

81   Belknap, pp. 182–183.

an order a commander must remain alert and make timely adjustments as required by a changing situation. The successful commander insures mission accomplishment through personal presence, observation and supervision. The military commander has complete and overall responsibility for all activities within his unit. He alone is responsible for everything his unit does or does not do. When troops commit massacres or atrocities against the civilian population of occupied territory or against prisoners of war, the responsibility may rest not only with the actual perpetrators but also with the commander."[82]

On the issue of responsibility and duty to report atrocities, the brief asserted a violation of Article 3 of the Geneva Convention. "A combat commander has a duty, both as an individual and as a commander, to insure that humane treatment is accorded to noncombatants and surrendering combatants. Additionally, all military personnel, regardless of rank or position, have the responsibility of reporting any incident or act thought to be a war crime to his commanding officer as soon as practicable after gaining such knowledge."[83]

The prosecution's case relied on the fact that Medina, as company commander, was in radio contact with his men in My Lai, was aware from the beginning that the units were receiving no hostile fire, and was aware his men were improperly killing noncombatants. The prosecution presented a weak case.

The defense, led by flamboyant civilian defense attorney F. Lee Bailey, was successful in getting any photographic evidence thrown out.

---

82 Prosecution brief on the Law of Principals in *United States v. Captain Ernest L. Medina*. Edwin Moïse's bibliography of My Lai, www.clemson.edu /caah/history/facultypages/Edmoise/mylai.html. Trial transcripts of the Trial of Ernest Medina.

83 Prosecution brief in *United States v. Captain Ernest L. Medina*. Edwin Moïse's bibliography of My Lai, www.clemson.edu/caah/history/facultypages/Edmoise/ mylai.html.

Bailey also asserted, as a defense, undue command influence; he alleged that superior officers were pressuring military authorities to reach a preordained conclusion of guilty because of all the pretrial publicity.

In his own defense, Medina denied knowing that his men had killed civilians, and by the end of the trial the judge had reduced the murder charge to involuntary manslaughter. Medina further claimed that his men had misunderstood his orders, and once he knew what was going on, he immediately ordered his men to cease fire. He also contended that he thought some of the civilian casualties were from the preinvasion artillery barrage.

It only took the jury of officers fifty-seven minutes to find Medina not guilty of all charges. It was not until several months later that Medina confessed that he had known all along that more than a hundred villagers had died, and only then did he admit he was "not completely candid" in statements he had made under oath to Army investigators. His reasons for these actions were his thoughts of the disgrace the truth would bring to the military, the United States, his family, and himself. But by then, being out of the Army, he could not be tried for perjury.[84]

---

84   Bilton and Sim, p. 349.

CHAPTER 7
Impact of the Verdict on the War Effort

THE reaction to the Calley verdict was swift and polarizing. Polls revealed overwhelming opposition to the conviction and sentence. Public opinion was so strong that President Richard M. Nixon intervened personally. The president ordered that Calley be allowed to remain in his barracks rather than the stockade pending his appeals.

With public opinion strongly in Calley's favor, public officials were scrambling to respond to the pressure to support him. The My Lai massacre and the Calley and Medina verdicts crystallized the conflicting views people held about the war. Hawks opposed the verdict because they thought Calley was being punished for waging a war they supported. They were upset at what they perceived as a soldier's being punished for trying to win the war. Doves, on the other hand, saw the verdict as an indictment of a war that should never have been fought in the first place. To them Calley became a symbol of a failed national policy. "The events of My Lai, for which Lieutenant Calley has been found guilty, are reflective of the tragedy of the entire Vietnam war," wrote Senator Abe Ribicoff, Democrat from Connecticut.[85]

The verdict no doubt accelerated what was an already declining level of support for the war. The American people were growing tired of a war that had no end in sight and no clear military objective. Nixon hoped to exploit the Calley conviction to generate support for the war, but those efforts failed.

Virtually everyone thought Calley was a scapegoat. For supporters of the war the guilty verdict was proof that the American troops were being prevented from doing what they had to do to win the war. They were frustrated by the fact that the war effort was limited to avoiding defeat rather than achieving victory. For opponents of the war the verdict symbolized everything that was wrong with the war. Calley was the scapegoat who took the rap for a failed policy. To them he was convicted for following orders—orders that included killing civilians. His conviction invigorated those who believed the war was the wrong policy and was needlessly taking the lives of American soldiers and innocent civilians. As confidence in the government continued to deteriorate, the Calley verdict only reinforced those doubts.

When the so-called Pentagon Papers were released on July 1, 1971, they revealed that government leaders had been lying to the American people about the war for many years. In light of those revelations, the Calley verdict became another example of government deceit and duplicity. To many, Calley was not a mass murderer but a victim of all they disliked and distrusted: the war, the system, and the government.[86]

The Calley case wound its way through the appellate system. His first appeal resulted in a reduction of his sentence to twenty years.

85   Belknap, p.210.
86   Belknap, p. 214.

Other appeals were denied until Federal District Judge J. Robert Elliot ordered Calley freed due to numerous violations of Calley's right to due process and a fair trial. According to Judge Elliot, prejudicial media coverage had precluded Calley's right to a fair trial. However, the Fifth Circuit overturned Judge Elliot's decision. In the meantime, Calley had become eligible for parole since Secretary of the Army Howard Calloway had reduced Calley's sentence to ten years. Calloway granted Calley's petition for parole, and on November 9, 1974, more than six years after My Lai, Calley was a free man.

Lieutenant William L. Calley was the only person convicted in the My Lai massacre even though dozens of soldiers had participated in the killings and dozens of officers had participated in the cover-up. Some members of Charlie Company who'd had charges pending found the charges dismissed before coming to trial thanks to the administrative review process. The process was used to discharge the soldiers from the Army and bar them from reenlistment.

As for others, Captain Medina was court-martialed and found innocent. The Army accused Captain Eugene Koutuc of assaulting and maiming a prisoner. It also filed murder charges against seven enlisted men: Sergeant Charles Hutto, Sergeant Esquiel Torres, Corporal Kenneth Schiel, SP-4 William F. Doherty, SP-4 Robert T'Souvas, Private Max D. Hutson, and Private Gerald Smith, all of whom participated in the massacre.[87] Others who had charges filed against them included the former commander of the American Division, Major General Koster. Also charged were Brigadier General George H. Young, Colonel Nels A. Parson, Colonel Oran Henderson, Colonel Robert B. Luper, Lieutenant Colonel David G. Garvin, Lieutenant Colonel William D. Guinn, Jr., Major Charles C. Calhoun, Major Frederick W.

---

87   Belknap, p. 217.

Watke, Captain Kenneth W. Boatman, Captain Dennis H. Johnson, Captain Thomas K. Willingham, and Major Robert W. McKnight.

Most of the charges against these persons stemmed from the cover-up, so these were primarily accusations of filing false statements or swearing falsely under oath.[88] Other than Calley, none were convicted. However, some of the officers' careers were seriously damaged when they were issued letters of censure and had their military decorations removed.[89]

The Army had little stomach for more public trials, which would only further erode public support for the war. As the Calley case faded from public view, the Army became less and less interested in pursuing these related cases. The next year, 1972, was a presidential election year, and by 1973 the country was engulfed in the Watergate scandal. My Lai had fallen off the public radar.

To its credit the post-Vietnam-era Army did address the shortcomings in training and leadership that the My Lai massacre exposed. By 1989, when the United States invaded Panama, military lawyers were involved in the planning process. Their involvement ensured that the restrictive rules of engagement were clear, that directives were issued to soldiers prohibiting the collection of "war trophies," and that soldiers were informed of the proper treatment of prisoners of war. In fact, by 1989, military lawyers had reviewed operational plans and provided legal advice to soldiers, before their deployment, on international law and the laws of war.

By Operation Desert Storm it had become common for military lawyers to be in the forefront. They thoroughly explained to soldiers about legal issues like contracts, claims, jurisdiction, the ban on alcohol in the armed forces, and the rules of engagement—all well prior to a

88   Belknap, p. 218.
89   Bilton and Sim, p. 351.

combat operation. The key difference from the Vietnam era is that military lawyers had become deeply involved in the war planning process. The operational law concept had finally taken hold in the US Army. Court-martial dealt swiftly with misbehaving service personnel, which sent a clear signal that discipline would be strictly enforced.[90]

The conflicts in Iraq and Afghanistan present similar challenges, and the dearth of major atrocities is evidence of an improving military justice system.

---

90 William T. Allison. *Military Justice in Vietnam: The Rule of Law in an American War.* Lawrence, Kansas: University Press of Kansas, 2007, pp. 179–181.

CHAPTER 8
Killer Team

BY 1968 there were approximately 55,000 US Marines stationed in the provinces surrounding Danang in northern South Vietnam. The III Marine Amphibious Force (III MAF) headquartered in Danang was responsible for the defense of the five northernmost provinces of South Vietnam. By all accounts this was hostile territory for the Marines. In those provinces were an estimated 78,000 enemy troops, including 49,000 North Vietnamese regulars, 6,000 Viet Cong regulars, and 23,000 VC guerillas.

Despite the numbers, by 1970 there were few large-scale engagements with the enemy. The Paris peace talks were under way, and the North Vietnamese had suffered severe losses in the Tet Offensive; so they now resorted to small hit-and-run attacks, mines, and terrorism. They saw this as a way to maintain their military position until the United States withdrew or the peace talks resulted in an agreement.[91]

Son Thang was a village in Quang Nam province, a stronghold of the Viet Minh since the defeat of the French in 1954. Quang Nam

---

91 Gary D. Solis. *Son Thang: An American War Crime.* New York: Bantam Books, 1997, pp. 9–10.

province was also allegedly the birthplace of Ho Chi Minh.[92] In many ways it was very similar to Quang Ngai. The people were supportive of the Viet Cong but eschewed politics. They were content to farm and take care of their ancestral homelands.

The First Marine Division was comprised of 28,000 men in four infantry regiments: the First, Fifth, Seventh, and Twenty-Sixth Marines; an artillery regiment, the Eleventh Marines; and several support battalions. Each regiment had three battalions of 1100 to 1200 men apiece and rotated between three patrol bases: Fire Support Base (FSB) Ryder, FSB Baldy, and FSB Ross.

FSB Ross commanded much of the Que Son Valley, which was among the most dangerous areas in South Vietnam. The situation was bad. Colonel Robert H. Barrow described it as, "Anything that moved you could shoot at because he was the enemy. You didn't have to separate the armed threat from the civilian population. Those Marines who went out there day after day conducting … combat patrols, almost knowing that somewhere on their route they were going to have some sort of surprise visited on them, either an ambush or explosive device … that is the worst kind of warfare, not being able to see the enemy. You can't shoot back at him. You are kind of helpless."[93]

The 1/7, short for First Battalion Seventh Marines, spent late 1969 in pursuit of the First and Third VC Regiments across Que Son. They were taking casualties on a regular basis. In November fifteen Marines were killed and eighty-four were wounded. In December another two Marines were lost and twenty were wounded. In January they bore the brunt of a vicious assault by VC forces that almost penetrated the

---

92   Denzil D. Garrison. *Honor Restored.* Mustang, Oklahoma: Tate Publishing, 2006, p. 145.

93   Solis, pp. 9–10 and 12–13.

camp's perimeter. The attack killed thirteen Marines and wounded sixty-three.

Afterward, the unit's commander was relieved of duty, and Lieutenant Colonel Charles G. Cooper assumed control of the battalion. He was the 1/7's third commander in five months. Cooper's first reaction upon assuming command was, "I was appalled … alcohol abuse, drug abuse, racial problems." The outfit was beset by poor discipline, low morale, and other problems.[94]

Among the members of the battalion was a young lieutenant named Louis R. Ambort. Ambort had been in Vietnam for only eight months before being promoted to first lieutenant. He was only twenty-three years old and had had only basic training. He was described as "aggressive" and "capable." He was also always very interested in the "Kill Board," which listed the number of enemy fighters killed each month. To Ambort it seemed that body counts mattered.

In December 1969, a new term had appeared in the 1/7's lexicon. Paragraph six of the 1/7's Organization and Operation chronology read: "Commencing 9 December 1969 companies started operating independently using platoon size patrols, squad size ambushes and killer teams." The chronology did not describe or define the term *killer teams*.[95]

In February 1970, B Company, part of the 1/7, was deployed to the area known as Son Thang 4, which was in the Que Son Valley. The South Vietnamese government used a system to denote the political affiliations of each village. Those with a 1 in their designated names were regarded as "all friendly." Those with the number 2 were "mostly friendly, some enemy." Those with the number 3 were "mostly enemy, some friendly." And logically, those with the number 4 were regarded

---

94   Solis, pp. 17–21.
95   Solis, pp. 16–17.

as "all enemy." The South Vietnamese government had designated Son Thang 4 as a village completely inhabited by Communist enemies and owned by the Viet Cong. It was known as "Indian Country" by the troops.[96]

Since October, Ambort, while leading B Company, had lost fourteen men with another eighty-four wounded. Nine were killed in just one week in February. On February 12, 1970, Sergeant Jerry E. Lineberry was ambushed and killed while on patrol. He had been a popular and well-respected Marine. A few days later the platoon lost Private First Class Richard Whitmore to a booby-trapped explosive mortar round. Ambort then decided to "send out one killer team."

Ambort and his second lieutenant, Bob Carney, found five volunteers: Lance Corporal Michael Krichten, and Privates First Class Thomas Boyd, Sam Green, Randy Herrod, and Michael Schwarz.

The team members all came from different backgrounds. Samuel G. Green, Jr., was the newest member of the platoon; he was also an African-American. He had only been in Vietnam twenty-nine days, and this was his first patrol. Prior to his enlistment he had had problems with the police in his hometown of Cleveland, Ohio. He had been convicted of incorrigibility, truancy, and running away. He also had a history of drug abuse and had spent three months in a juvenile detention center. His record in the Marine Corps at that point had been exemplary.

Boyd and Krichten both had two years of high school and had enlisted in August 1969. They had served together and formed the sort of strong bond common for soldiers who have shared combat experiences. Each had been wounded in combat.

Michael A. Schwarz was from rural Pennsylvania and at twenty-one was the oldest member of the squad. He had one year of high

---

96   Garrison, p. 146.

school under his belt. He had been in Vietnam for four months and had considerable combat experience. Though, Schwarz was not a model soldier. He had been disciplined for being drunk in camp and was considered for an administrative discharge because of his "unfitness." In normal times he would have been discharged based on his frequent conflicts with military authorities. However, in 1970 in Vietnam, the need for bodies was so pressing that discharge was unlikely. He was also carrying a stolen M-16.

Private Randall Dean Herrod was part Creek Indian and came from Calvin, Oklahoma. He enlisted in 1968 and was sent to Vietnam in 1969. He was originally assigned to Third Battalion of the Third Marines as an assistant machine gunner.

While serving in Company K 3/3, Herrod's team was attacked by an NVA force. He was wounded by shrapnel but continued to fight. When he saw a young lieutenant get blown off a tank, Herrod climbed out of the protection of his foxhole to rescue the lieutenant, dragging him to safety. While protecting the wounded officer, Herrod fired his M-60 machine gun to hold off the enemy advance.

The lieutenant then ran out of the hole and back to the command tank. A shell exploded with such force that the officer was thrown into the air, and again Herrod climbed out of his foxhole into an exposed position to drag his lieutenant to safety. He was awarded the Silver Star for his actions in the field that day. The lieutenant was Oliver L. North, and he credited Herrod with saving his life.

Herrod was later promoted to lance corporal, after which he went AWOL for two months, hanging out in Danang, going to clubs, and partying. After he ran out of money, he turned himself in to await disciplinary action. In light of his combat record and the need for combat soldiers, Herrod received a light sentence of a reduction in rank, a seventy-dollar fine, and three months hard labor probated, meaning he served no time in the brig.[97] He was returned to Bravo Company and Lieutenant Ambort's command.

On February 20, 1970, Herrod was placed in charge of the killer team. He was not the highest-ranking member of the team. However, Sergeant Harvey Meyers and Lieutenant Carney felt he was the best suited of the men to lead the team, given his combat experience. By this time in Vietnam there was an acute shortage of experienced noncommissioned officers. Often authority was derived from position occupied rather than rank. The term *bush rank* became popular, meaning leaders who often emerged from situations that had little to do with actual rank. Lieutenant Colonel Cooper noted, "This type of small unit jury-rigging was not unusual … In my opinion, the problem started here. It was a judgmental error of considerable magnitude."[98] Certainly Herrod's selection was influenced by his prior recommendation for a Silver Star.

After assembling, the team met with Lieutenant Ambort and Sergeant Meyers to receive their final briefing. The plan was to go to Hill 270, where they had encountered enemy soldiers before. It was a circular route that would bring them right back to the base. Ambort gave them a pep talk: "I told him I didn't want any casualties … Since they were out there alone, there wouldn't be much I could do. And I emphasized the fact to him [Herrod] not to take any chances, to shoot first and ask questions later. I reminded him of the nine people that we had killed on February 12, and I reminded him of Whitmore, who had died that day. I said, 'Don't let them get us any more. I want you to pay these little bastards back.'"

---

97   Solis, pp. 40–44.
98   Solis, pp. 28–29.

Krichten recalled the pep talk as meaning "to go out and kill as many of the enemy as we could."

Boyd recalled, "Kill anything moving around."

Schwarz heard, "Kill any gooks in the area."[99]

Herrod said, "I told him I understood him perfectly. We were all ready to get our pound of flesh."[100]

Son Thang 4 was only few hundred meters from Fire Support Base Ross. The soldiers and civilians alike understood that a dusk-to-dawn curfew was in effect for all Vietnamese civilians. As far as the killer team understood the rules of engagement, if people were out at night, they were fair game. Additionally, Son Thang was on the boundary of a free-fire zone—a designated area established by the South Vietnamese government as preapproved for the employment of military fire and maneuvers because it was free of civilians. Since the Viet Cong lived among the rural population, the theory was that if the population were relocated, whoever remained must be a VC. However, many rural Vietnamese had not relocated for fear of losing their homes and spiritual history. Unfortunately, villagers who remained were often considered to be VC sympathizers regardless of their political feelings (if any).[101]

The killer team approached the village, wary of any enemy threat, knowing full well that the area was not sympathetic to American troops. At the first checkpoint, they reached a hooch, a small hut of the type in which most rural Vietnamese resided. Herrod ordered Schwartz to enter the hooch. It was empty. They approached a second hooch twenty-five meters away, from which they heard voices. Boyd circled

99   Solis, p. 30.
100   Randy Herrod. *Blue's Bastards: A True Story of Valor Under Fire.* Washington, DC: Regnery Publishing, 1989, p. 136.
101   Solis, pp. 45–47.

around the back to block any escape while Schwarz and the others stood at the front. Herrod ordered Schwarz to call out the occupants.

Four Vietnamese slowly emerged from the hooch: an old woman, a younger woman, and two girls. The younger woman was blind. According to Krichten's account, Schwarz then went inside to search the hooch while the remaining Marines guarded the women. While inside, Schwarz heard Herrod yell, "Shoot them, shoot them all! Kill them!"[102]

Krichten claimed that Schwarz came out of the hooch, the older woman ran for the trees, and Herrod shot her with an M-79. She was wounded, and Herrod ordered Schwarz to "go over and finish her off," which he did by shooting her twice with his .45-caliber pistol.

Krichten later testified that Herrod ordered them to kill the remaining three. The Marines complied, and all four females were shot at close range with automatic weapons. The oldest was fifty; the youngest was five years old.

At this point the soldiers heard voices from the first hooch, which they had found empty. Going back to investigate, they found inside six Vietnamese who had emerged from a bunker inside the hooch. Once again the occupants were all women and children. Suddenly Private Green shouted that one of the women was reaching for something in her waistband. Green fired a single shot, presumably, but no one was hit. The children began to cry. According to Krichten, Herrod ordered the Marines into a single line and ordered them to shoot: "I want these people killed immediately." Then everybody started firing. All six were killed; their ages ranged from forty-three to three years old.

Moving back toward the tree line to begin the journey back to base, the team encountered a third hooch. They surrounded the hooch and called out the occupants. Six Vietnamese women emerged and stood

102 Solis, p. 49.

in front of the hooch. According to Krichten, one of the soldiers fired an M-79, and then Herrod hollered, "Shoot them, kill them, kill them all! Kill all of them bitches!"

Everybody opened up with gunfire into the assembled group of women and children. When they stopped, they heard a child crying, and Herrod ordered Schwarz to finish the child off, which he did with his .45. The team then returned to base, having killed sixteen Vietnamese women and children.[103]

---

103 Solis, pp. 49–53.

CHAPTER 9
Investigation

UPON returning to base the team was immediately debriefed. Given the proximity of the base camp to the village, those at camp had heard and recognized the familiar sound of M-16s firing on automatic. Herrod claimed they had killed six Viet Cong in an ambush but later admitted he lied in his debriefing: "It was a lie, or at best a half truth; I would live to regret it. But at the moment I didn't have the heart to tell him we probably hadn't killed any Cong, though we might have blown away some women and children."[104]

Lieutenant Ambort may have had his suspicions as there were no weapons captured, although when making his report to his superiors he offered one that the battalion had captured previously in order to buttress the team's report. Ambort submitted his report to his superiors. Within days the company operations officer, Major Dick Theer, who initially congratulated Ambort on the success of the mission, wanted more information. Ambort again asked the team what really happened, and according to Krichten, Herrod and he told Ambort they had

---

104   Herrod, p. 140.

killed women and children but only after having been fired upon first. Ambort concluded the killings were justified because the Vietnamese had been violating curfew and had fired on the team first.

The next day First Lieutenant Floyd Grant, intelligence officer for the First Battalion Seventh Marines, was approached while on patrol by a Vietnamese woman who complained that Americans had entered her hamlet the night before and had killed many women and children. Grant went to the site and discovered the bodies of the dead Vietnamese. All had been killed by gunshots at close range. The empty shell casings were all from M-16 rifles, M-79 fire, and .45-caliber pistols. Grant's discovery triggered a new round of reports and queries. Coming on the heels of the Army massacre at My Lai, the Marine Corps would waste no time investigating this alleged atrocity. Major Theer was assigned the task of investigating the alleged crime.

Theer immediately issued Article 31 warnings to Lieutenant Ambort and each member of the team before interviewing them. An Article 31 warning mandates that a soldier be provided advance notice when suspected of a crime. Similar to a Miranda warning in the civilian system, an Article 31 permits a suspected soldier to remain silent and have counsel assigned immediately and to have said counsel present during any interview.

Starting with Herrod, Theer invited the suspects, one by one, to explain the events of the incident. Herrod declined counsel and told Theer they had been fired upon during the patrol. He said the civilians had been killed in the cross fire and may have participated in the shooting. Herrod was instructed to put his account in writing, which he did. He said that while the squad members were interrogating the women a shot zinged over their heads, one woman ran, and the soldiers returned fire. At the second hooch, again two shots were fired in their direction; the soldiers had shot the occupants because they were part of the setup. The occupants of the third hooch were likewise involved in the ambush and killed.

Private Boyd was interviewed next, and his account paralleled Herrod's. He too put his account in writing, although he said that at the third hooch there was no incoming fire. But once one Marine started firing, they all followed suit.

At this point, Lieutenant Ambort now admitted his report was false, that the men had lied to him, and that the recovered weapon was from a prior patrol. Theer began to realize the situation was far more serious than he had thought earlier.

Private Green's statement was identical to Herrod's and Boyd's, except he admitted that he had been the one to fire first at the third hooch. The remaining two members of the team relayed similar stories, yet Schwarz and Krichten requested the opportunity to rewrite and revise their written statements. Schwarz did state that at the first hooch they shot the women and children because they thought they were part of a trap, as they did at the second hooch. At the third, once Green fired, Herrod ordered them all to fire.

Something was amiss. The statements were too contrived, and yet all admitted killing civilians without provocation. Theer took a team to the village where the killings had taken place to ascertain the veracity of the statements. He was looking for some evidence of an ambush or sniper within range of the village that could corroborate the Marines' story that they were fired upon. He found no such evidence.

Theer again issued Article 31 warnings to the team and summoned them for interviews, this time with Criminal Investigation Command staff present. Herrod relied on his written statement. He admitted he was worried about what Boyd or Krichten would say since he did not know them as well as the others.

His concern was justified. Boyd then admitted under questioning that there was no sniper fire that evening. Boyd retracted his earlier statement and wrote a new one. He wrote that Herrod had ordered the killings. "We hesitated and he insisted we kill them. Same thing at the second hooch and third hooch. We did not receive sniper fire as far as I know, and I am truly sorry I had a hand in it."[105]

Lance Corporal Krichten also recanted his earlier statement and wrote, "There was no sniper fire, and there weren't any enemy ... Herrod said to open up on all these people ... I didn't think it was right at all."

Green did not recant his earlier statement; he was hostile and said, "What do I care about some gook woman or child! It's them or me. If they get in my way, that's too bad!"

Schwarz then recanted his prior statement and wrote a new one. He said, "He was searching the hooches, Herrod ordered all the civilians herded up and killed. The same at each hooch. He fired along with everyone else; although they hesitated, we were ordered to fire and did. He said the team leader told them they received sniper fire, which the men agreed to repeat if asked."[106]

All five members of the killer team were charged with the premeditated murder of sixteen noncombatant civilians.

---

105   Solis, pp. 80-81
106   Solis, pp. 77–84.

CHAPTER 10
Court-martial

IMMEDIATELY after charges were filed, Krichten cut a deal with the prosecution to testify against his comrades in return for full immunity from prosecution.

The trials were all held in Danang, under relatively primitive conditions, with little press coverage. The courtroom was small by military base standards, the air conditioning was erratic, and there was little access to legal libraries. There is no transcribed record of the Herrod or Boyd trials.

Schwarz was the first to go on trial. Counsel assigned by the Marines represented him. Captain Dan LeGear led the Schwarz defense team. By this time, news of the prosecutions had reached the United States, and like with the Calley trial, some people, particularly friends and family of the accused, solicited support for their defense.

In the case of Randy Herrod, his situation attracted the attention of two prominent criminal defense attorneys from his hometown of Wewoka, Oklahoma. Denzil D. Garrison was a state senator in Oklahoma and was good friends with Herrod's uncle, Gene Short.

Garrison was a Korean War veteran and at the time was the Republican floor leader of the Oklahoma Senate.

Garrison reached out to another state senator, Gene Stipe, who had a reputation for being an outstanding trial lawyer. They were good friends and colleagues and the odd couple of the Oklahoma Senate, as Garrison was a conservative Republican and Stipe was a liberal Democrat. At their own expense, they assembled a defense team and set out for Danang to represent Randy Herrod. Before, they sat in the gallery and observed the Schwarz trial. The judge for this trial was a Marine, Lieutenant Colonel Paul A. St. Amour. The prosecutor was Captain Franz P. Jevne, who would also be prosecuting Herrod.

LeGear's pretrial strategy was to exclude as much evidence as possible, but he lost every motion, including one to exclude photographs of the dead civilians. Schwarz's damaging statements to Theer were also admitted. A jury was seated comprised of Marine officers with extensive infantry experience.

The prosecution's case was built around Schwarz's own admissions in his statements to Theer and the testimony of Lance Corporal Michael Krichten. The jury heard Krichten testify to seeing Schwarz shooting the people at the first and third hooches. Krichten was less confident about the second hooch and said he himself had fired over the peoples' heads. The jury also heard testimony from Sergeant Harvey Meyers who had helped assemble the team.

The defense tried to establish that Schwarz was simply following orders and that civilians were often combatants in Vietnam, but Krichten damaged Schwarz's case badly. He testified to seeing Schwarz kill the civilians and execute a wounded woman and a small child at close range. Lieutenant Ambort also testified for the defense and described the dangers inherent in that area and the many instances in which women and children had participated in ambushes and attacks on Marines.

But even with Ambort's testimony, by all accounts Schwarz was in trouble. Herrod's attorneys watched in horror as the prosecution and judge moved swiftly toward a conviction.[107] The "just following orders" defense had been discredited since Nuremberg. The judge advised the jury that the justification of following orders does not exist when the act done is manifestly beyond the scope of the senior officer's authority or when the order is of such a nature that a man of ordinary sense and understanding would know it to be illegal.[108] The jury found Private Michael Schwarz guilty of premeditated murder on twelve specifications and acquitted him of four specifications. He was sentenced to life imprisonment with forfeit of all pay and allowances and given dishonorable discharge from the Marine Corps.[109]

Herrod had offered to testify for Schwarz but was rebuffed. In his account he claimed that the others "were ignorant of the true sequence of events. Since their lawyers did not interview me but proceeded to build a defense without the true story no one really had enough information to put together a legitimate defense based on the fact we had been fired on and were protecting our lives."[110]

Next up were Boyd and Green. Boyd had civilian counsel along with a military lawyer. Howard Trockman was an outspoken critic of the war from Boyd's hometown of Evansville, Indiana. He too had observed the Schwarz trial and recognized the need to alter his defense strategy. For one, he decided to forego a jury and have a bench trial,

107　Garrison, pp. 98–99.
108　Solis, p. 201.
109　Garrison, p. 99.
110　Herrod, p. 161.

meaning the judge alone would determine guilt or innocence. In this case St. Amour was again the presiding judge. However, a different prosecutor was assigned; Captain Charles E. Brown, Jr., who had been second chair in the Schwarz case, would lead the prosecution team.

Brown pursued a similar strategy to his predecessor as he successfully introduced the photographs and the statements into the record. Krichten and Meyers testified as well, and this time his testimony contained a surprising twist. Krichten and Boyd were close friends. They had been together for almost seven months in Vietnam, fighting together in many combat situations. Krichten recalled that Boyd was a pacifist and often did not fire his weapon in combat. He testified that Boyd had fired his weapon over the heads of the victims at Son Thang. Killing is difficult for most people; killing at close range can be even more difficult, he explained.

The government could not rebut Krichten's testimony. Without ballistics or eyewitness testimony the government could not prove Boyd had killed anyone at Son Thang. Boyd's defense elaborated on Krichten's testimony by establishing that Boyd was a religious man who had joined the Marines only to prove to his mother that he was a man. He said he waited until the victims at Son Thang had fallen before firing his weapon. He had only fired so his comrades would not think he was a coward.

Herrod felt Boyd was lying but did not blame him for trying.[111] St. Amour found Boyd not guilty on all charges, explaining that he felt Boyd had played a role in the killings and had probably shot some of the victims, but the prosecution had not been able to establish his guilt beyond a reasonable doubt.[112]

Green also had a civilian defense attorney, James A. Chiara.

111   Herrod, p. 163.
112   Solis, p. 223.

His military attorney was Captain John J. Hargrove. Green was an angry man who had had numerous run-ins with the law as a youth in Cleveland, Ohio. He was the only African-American on the killer team. Like many of his generation, Green was given a choice between enlisting in the armed forces and going to jail. He was an individual replacement at Son Thang; he was new and had no previous combat experience and no connection to the unit.

St. Amour again presided over the trial, and Green opted for a jury of military personnel. Brown was the prosecutor, and the case followed the same pattern as the previous two trials. The photos and pretrial statements were all admitted. Green was charged with unpremeditated murder, sixteen counts. Krichten testified that Green had fired at all three hooches. Green's statements that he fired after seeing the woman reach into her waistband were incriminating.

The defense alleged that Herrod and Schwarz were the ringleaders, and Green himself testified that he purposely tried to miss when he fired his weapon. He only fired under Herrod's repeated orders. No mention was made of any enemy fire. The defense claimed Green's inexperience led him to make an error in judgment; plus, no one testified that they saw any particular victim hit by Green's rifle. Even so, the jury found him guilty on all counts. The jury sentenced him to a rank reduction to private, loss of all pay and allowances, dishonorable discharge, and five years' imprisonment.[113] No explanation was given for the disparity in the sentences between Green and Schwarz. It could be that the jury considered Green's lack of combat experience as a mitigating factor in determining a fair sentence.

The final trial was that of Randy Herrod. Herrod had a few distinct advantages compared to his cohorts. His civilian legal team was outstanding. They were experienced and savvy and had the benefit

---

113   Solis, pp. 232–236.

of observing the three previous trials, so they knew exactly what to expect from the prosecution.

Additionally, Judge St. Amour was abruptly transferred to Iwakuna, Japan, so the presiding judge for Herrod's hearing was Navy Commander Keith Lawrence. Like the previous trials, the defense team sought to exclude the pictures via a pretrial motion to exclude. This time they forced the prosecution to explain the probative value of the photos. The prosecutor, Charles Brown, explained that the photos would show the locations of the bodies, the positions of the cartridges, and the ages of the deceased. The defense promptly stipulated to all those items, agreeing with the prosecution as to the photos showing that information. By doing so this eliminated any need to admit the photos as evidence, and the judge sustained the defense's motion to exclude the photos. To the extent that a photo is worth a thousand words, this was a big win for Herrod, as the pictures were very damaging.[114]

Herrod opted for a jury trial, and his jury consisted entirely of Marine officers. In addition to his civilian lawyers, he had a military attorney, Captain Robert C. Williams, also a Marine. Garrison and Stipe mounted a defense primarily on the premise that the patrol was fired upon and had acted in self-defense.

The prosecution called Sergeant Harvey Meyers to the stand first, as it had in the previous trials. Meyers, who had briefed the team before they had gone to Son Thang, testified that he heard automatic weapons fire from the village that night, specifically, American M-60 machine gunfire. He also testified that the team had had no such weapon with them that night. This was news to the prosecution; no one had asked him that question before.

Intelligence officer Lieutenant Grant was called to recount his discovery of the bodies and the locations of the shell casings. Only

114 Garrison, pp. 135–136.

shell casings from American weaponry were found, specifically M-16s, .45-calibers, and M-79s.

Next Krichten was called to the stand for the fourth time. He repeated his testimony about Ambort's briefing and his directions to "get some." He described the shootings at the three hooches as well as his protests to Boyd about shooting the women and children at the first hut and at Herrod's shooting a woman with his M-79 grenade launcher then telling Schwarz to finish her off. He also told the jury that Herrod had ordered the people killed. On cross-examination Krichten was asked about a wound he had suffered to his neck by a spent round. He admitted to being hurt and that the round *could* have come from an enemy weapon, since no one in the patrol could have hit him.

Gary Solis and Denzil Garrison disagreed on the impact of Krichten's testimony. Garrison called it "craven and furtive,"[115] while Solis found it "impressive."[116] Considering the prosecution's case relied heavily on Krichten's testimony, the fact that the defense found him unpersuasive is important. Obviously their analysis was correct. After only seven witnesses the prosecution rested its case. In this case, the prosecution had difficulty refuting the defense argument that the team had been fired upon before opening fire themselves. After hearing Krichten testify that he could have been wounded by an enemy round, the prosecution should have been prepared for a more robust defense presentation regarding the possible presence of enemy troops nearby.

The defense was well prepared and presented some critical evidence heretofore not known to the prosecution. They called Sergeant Bruce Fay, who testified that he had been on patrol ten days after the incident at Son Thang and had come under fire from a machine gun located somewhere on a hill immediately behind the village. He described

115 Garrison, p. 175.
116 Solis, p. 265.

the weapon as an M-60 machine gun. He described how his patrol pinpointed the gunfire's location as being in a cave and how they had assaulted the cave with grenades and small weapons fire. After killing the Viet Cong manning the gun they retrieved the gun and determined that the weapon had been stolen from a helicopter gunship that had been shot down several months past. The gun had been pointed toward Son Thang.

The next witness, Sergeant Ron Butler, brought the M-60 into the courtroom and identified it as the captured machine gun. This testimony was very damaging to the prosecution, and interestingly, the prosecution never introduced the statements from Boyd, Schwarz, and Green, who had all said there was no enemy fire that evening. Even Herrod's statement only mentioned three bullets.

The defense then called former battalion commander Charles G. Cooper, who gave the usual testimony about the inherent dangers in and around Son Thang. Next the defense called Lieutenant Oliver North to testify to Herrod's courage under fire and his heroics the night he had saved North's life. North's testimony was "effective," according to Garrison.[117]

Herrod then took the stand in his own defense. He stuck to his story that the patrol had been fired upon; however, on cross-examination he was forced to admit he had originally lied to Lieutenant Ambort when they returned from the mission. Other than his response that he was scared and wanted to please his lieutenant, Herrod remained unshaken and stuck to his story.

The defense called a psychiatrist, Dr. Hayden M. Donahue, who would testify on the effects of "battle fatigue" on combat soldiers. Donahue testified that Herrod was probably suffering from battle fatigue the night of the killings, since he had been in combat for

---

117 Garrison, p. 188.

months, had seen his friends killed, and had faced death on a daily basis. He explained that Herrod's reasoning had been replaced by instinct.[118]

Donahue's testimony was helpful to the defense, and the prosecution had no refuting medical testimony to offer. On rebuttal, the prosecution was unable to challenge the suddenly found machine gun, though Theer had testified in earlier trials that he personally had investigated the scene and found no way for the enemy to have fired on the Marines that night. Theer was even called to testify in rebuttal in Herrod's trial but was never asked to refute the testimony of Fay and Butler.[119]

The case went to the jury. After three hours of deliberation the jury found Randy Herrod not guilty on all counts.

Many factors led to this unusual and surprising set of verdicts. It cannot be understated that the quality of the lawyers made a huge difference in the outcomes. Herrod was lucky to have a brilliant team of defense lawyers who had the time and resources to build a strong defense. He was also fortunate to be the last of the four tried, which gave his team a big advantage in preparation. The prosecution in his case seemed to have been overconfident and unprepared for the testimonies of Butler, Fay, and Dr. Donahue. The prosecution had also underestimated the relationship between Boyd and Krichten and had relied too heavily on Krichten's testimony, which ultimately exonerated Boyd. As Solis points out, the issue is not always whether the defendant committed the crime as it is whether the prosecution can prove beyond a reasonable doubt that he did it.[120]

The problem with the Herrod verdict is that it simply does not comport with the testimony. Herrod claimed in his defense that the

---

118   Solis, p. 278.
119   Garrison, p. 197.
120   Solis, p. 291.

squad was fired upon and that the civilians were killed in the cross fire. Not only was there no evidence of an actual firing on the patrol's position that night, but the locations of the bodies and their conditions were clear evidence that they were not incidental victims of a firefight.

Lieutenant Grant testified that the bodies were found in piles in front of each hooch. They were killed by small arms fire at close range. Were there a firefight, would the civilians not have been found in various locations, seeking cover from the incoming rounds? At least one hooch had a bunker, so it stands to reason that civilians would have been hiding were there a gun battle taking place in the village. Secondly, the civilians were killed by M-16, .45-caliber, and M-79 rounds; no M-60 shell casings were ever located. Had the victims been killed in a cross fire would not at least some of them suffered wounds from the alleged M-60 machine gun? Herrod's team did not reconcile his own statement that a bullet whizzed over his head with the fact that a machine gun fires hundreds of rounds a minute.

Solis raises the issue of whether the jury fell prey to the "mere gook rule" and was lenient with Herrod because of his prior heroism and the ongoing difficulty of distinguishing friend from foe in Vietnam. Solis offered one explanation for the lenient verdict quoting Guenter Lewy: "If officers serving on court-martial acquitted defendants or adjudged light sentences, their verdicts much of the time were the result of sympathy they felt for the frustrations experienced by the men ... a tendency to close ranks and to protect fellow officers or comrades-in-arms from the enlisted ranks."[121] To Solis the acquittals of Boyd and Herrod reflect the unpredictable course of particular cases in any legal system. To the credit of the Marine Corps there was no cover-up or official misconduct in the handling of these cases.

By way of postscript, Schwarz ultimately had his sentence reduced

---

121 Solis, p. 291.

to one year in prison. He was released from prison on April 2, 1971. Meanwhile, Green's initial appeals were all denied, but a young Marine, James H. Webb, Jr., took up his cause. An Annapolis graduate and Vietnam veteran, Webb attended Georgetown Law School after being medically retired from the Marines. Webb persisted on Green's behalf, alleging among other things that race played a role in Green's harsh sentence. Webb pursued appeals for Green and in 1978 succeeded in getting Green's dishonorable discharge overturned into a general discharge. Part of the argument was that Green had just been following orders, and the individual who had given the orders and killed some of the people had been exonerated.

The upgraded discharge was sent to Green's mother in 1978. Unfortunately, Green had shot and killed himself in 1975 after the Ohio Federal Court had refused to overturn his conviction.[122]

Webb went on to become Secretary of the Navy under President Ronald Reagan and is, at the time of this writing, a Democratic US senator representing Virginia.

---

122 Solis, pp. 328–329.

CHAPTER 11
American Conscience

THE broader impact of the My Lai and Son Thang incidents on the war effort and public support for the war is difficult to gauge. The Calley trial began as support for the war had begun to wane. The increasing number of casualties with little battlefield success undermined the perception that the United States was winning the war. Protests on college campuses, which had been a common occurrence, grew more violent each week. The outcome of the judicial process, which resulted in the conviction of only Calley, led many to believe that the Army had failed to bring those responsible to account and that Calley had suffered an injustice by being the scapegoat for the failures of his superiors.

Ironically it was Calley who became the object of public sympathy, not his victims. Though as Kendrick Oliver points out, while the American debates about the massacre were impassioned and inclusive of much of the national community, they were not sufficient to force the country to conscience.[123] For many Americans the origins of the atrocities committed by American troops in Vietnam lay in the broader

---

123   Kendrick Oliver. *The My Lai Massacre in American History and Memory.* Manchester, UK: Manchester University Press, 2006, p. 10.

culture of American war making. Many felt these atrocities were simply a reflection of a failed war effort and a misguided policy promoted by self-serving generals and politicians.

My Lai drew comparisons to the atrocities committed by the Germans in World War II. Some researchers believe that with respect to both My Lai and the Vietnam War as a whole, many American citizens—like the citizens of Germany as the Holocaust gathered speed—had simply decided that the killing of innocents did not merit their concern.[124]

If anything, My Lai and Son Thang only hardened people's feelings about the war. Those who favored it saw these trials as tools of the left-wing doves who sought to undermine the American war effort. The defendants were victims, hometown kids who were getting railroaded for following orders and fighting for their country. Those who already opposed the war saw these incidents as a validation of their opposition to a neocolonialist foreign policy that was doomed from the beginning. Out-of-control soldiers were murdering innocent people to advance a failed policy.

In the case of Randy Herrod, his two primary defense attorneys reflected exactly that paradox. Stipe, a liberal, antiwar Democrat, and Garrison, a conservative, pro-war Republican, joined forces for different reasons to defend Herrod. Frank Reynolds, a correspondent for ABC News, remarked that the disclosure of the atrocity at My Lai "offer[s] the most compelling argument yet advanced for America to end its involvement in Vietnam, not alone because of what the war is doing to the Vietnamese or to our reputation abroad, but because of what it is doing to us."[125]

The root causes of these massacres lie in myriad factors that all

---

124 Oliver, p. 137.
125 Oliver, p. 228.

seemed to converge on My Lai and Son Thang. Most of the troops involved were draftees. They were trained to kill and to follow orders. They had little interest in military history and had little loyalty to their battalion or division. They were primarily interested in surviving twelve months in Vietnam. They were loyal to their fellow soldiers and developed strong bonds among their peers on that level. Many times, officers were not held in high regard, particularly Calley.

The military fostered a culture of disrespect for the Vietnamese. The "mere gook rule" did little to encourage respect or understanding between soldiers and civilians. Vietnamese were referred to as "gooks," "dinks," or "slopes." Military brass did nothing to change that culture.

Body counts became the metric for success or failure. Killing was the way companies received recognition. Civilian casualties were just another part of the war. "Anything that's dead and isn't white is a VC" was a common refrain.[126] These men would spend months in the jungle going out on patrols and losing comrades every day to land mines, snipers, and booby traps. They were scared and wary of everyone and everything. Women and children were often used to plant mines and booby traps.

The soldiers involved in both massacres were in known Viet Cong strongholds. They were literally surrounded by hostiles, yet they rarely saw the enemy or had a pitched battle. They were ill-equipped and unprepared for a guerilla war. By the time Charlie Company reached My Lai they were pumped up to avenge their lost friends. Everything fell apart, and the company lost all sense of perspective and control.

All of these factors may explain why the incidents happened but do not in any way justify them. There is no explanation or excuse for the

126   Seymour M. Hersh. *My Lai 4: A Report on the Massacre and Its Aftermath.* New York: Random House, 1970, pp. 55–56.

widespread sexual assaults and the deliberate execution of women and children who posed no threat to the men. Charlie Company was not the only company in Vietnam to lose men to booby traps and snipers. Why did these guys commit these atrocities and not others? Why did Herrod's killer team murder sixteen civilians while other Marine patrols did no such thing? Why did some shoot and others refuse to participate? How is it that Hugh Thompson summoned up the courage to end an atrocity while others stood by and did nothing?

The war in Vietnam was a war to prevent Communist aggression. North Vietnam, supported by Communist China and the Soviet Union, invaded South Vietnam to expand its territory and unify the country under a Communist regime. The United States was determined to prevent that take over. Ideology played little role in the training of the military for service in Vietnam. Thus the massacres at My Lai and Son Thang had no ideological component.

CHAPTER 12
War and Murder

ATROCITIES committed in wartime have generated considerable debate, whether or not ideology was the driving force behind the killings. The most common comparison to the Vietnam incidents is the experience of the Nazi Army and police during World War II. The murder of millions of Jews and others during the Nazi occupation of Eastern Europe is well documented. German Army units and the Nazi police battalions comprised of ordinary German citizens carried out most of the killings. To what extent were these Germans motivated to murder innocent civilians by Nazi ideology? Is ideology a necessary predicate to mass murder?

In his book *Ordinary Men*, Christopher Browning describes a Nazi police battalion comprised of middle-class Germans from Hamburg stationed in Poland in 1942 and 1943. This reserve police battalion, whose members ranged in age from thirty-three to forty-eight, murdered thousands of Jewish men, women, and children, often by shooting them at close range.[127]

Browning's theory is that they were motivated by mundane concerns for acceptance and conformity within a larger group. He saw them as being motivated not by fanatical adherence to National Socialism but by respect and deference to authority, concern for career advancement, and peer group pressure.[128] Interestingly, many of the men experienced bouts of depression and guilt similar to ones felt by the American soldiers at My Lai. Also, some of the Germans refused to participate in the killings, preferring to stay on the perimeter and observe while others did the killing.

Browning makes the argument that war, and especially race war, leads to brutalization. He includes My Lai with other wartime atrocities, such as Babi Yar, New Guinea, Bromberg, and Malmedy. However, he points out that many wartime atrocities like those and others have been described by historians as "battlefield frenzy." Soldiers were inured to violence, numbed to the taking of human life, embittered over their own casualties, and frustrated by a mysterious enemy.[129]

While the military leadership may have tolerated these atrocities, they were not condoned and did not reflect official military policy. On the other hand, sometimes the killing of civilians was official policy, such as the firebombings of Dresden and Tokyo and the reprisal shootings in occupied Nazi territory. These actions are calculated and do not fall within the category of battlefield frenzy.

The ability of a perpetrator to dehumanize and distance themselves from the killing is the key factor in facilitating the mass murder of innocents. Browning sees distancing as the key to explaining the actions

127 Browning, pp. 1–2.
128 Westermann, p. 6.
129 Browning, p. 160.

of Reserve Police Battalion 101.[130] As they became uncomfortable with the increasing brutality of their actions they began to parse out their duties so they would be on the periphery of the killing. For the larger mass killings they would provide the transportation to the killing fields and create the cordon, but "specialists" brought in to deliver the fatal shots did the actual killing. This division of labor was "desensitizing" and allowed the members of the brigade to rationalize their actions. These individuals were not selected because of their commitment to the Nazi ideology; in fact, they were the least likely candidates to become mass murderers.

Daniel Goldhagen, in his book *Hitler's Willing Executioners*, argues that ordinary Germans easily became genocidal killers because German culture was anti-Semitic. Goldhagen sees a German culture and society rife with anti-Semites, such that the German people were easily persuaded to become genocidal murderers.[131]

But Goldhagen may have oversimplified the issue by building his case on the singular premise that the Holocaust occurred because all Germans hated Jews. Edward B. Westermann argues that Browning minimizes ideology, while Goldhagen overstates his case that ideology was the driving force behind the Holocaust. He sees a middle ground where the motivation for mass murder went beyond just ideology. Westermann sees a German society that became militarized by the Nazi culture. National Socialism was not just a political movement; it was a cultural phenomenon that extended into every aspect of German life. It pervaded the entire social fabric of German society: the arts, media, popular culture, sports, family life, and government. The tone was aggressive while the people were bombarded with propaganda on

---

130 Browning, pp. 161–162.
131 Daniel J. Goldhagen. *Hitler's Willing Executioners, Ordinary Germans and the Holocaust,* New York: Vintage Books, 1996, p. 23.

the virtues of military duty and sacrifice. This included references to the German master race and the need for space so the German people could expand their influence.

Westermann's conclusion is that the Nazi Army and the citizen police embarked on a campaign of premeditated annihilation sanctioned from the very highest levels of political, civil, and military leadership. In the course of creating a German empire, Himmler's SS existed in an organizational environment that created a "new moral order," one in which principles of exclusion and enmity such as anti-Semitism and anti-Bolshevism reigned supreme.[132]

The concept of political soldiers is not novel, considering historians have wrestled with this issue for many years. To what extent can an army become a political organization, and how can soldiers be trained to carry out unspeakable atrocities in the advancement of that political agenda? Omer Bartov outlines several factors that explain the willingness of the *Wehrmacht* to engage in flagrant atrocities against noncombatants on both the eastern and western fronts in World War II. He ascribes long years of ideological training to help soldiers overcome their moral scruples. The German soldier was not expected to become ideologically committed to Nazi dogma; however, the central themes of Nazi ideology—racism, anti-Semitism, anti-capitalism, anti-Bolshevism, and the creation of *Lebensraum* in the east, as well as the construction of a racially pure people at home—had much support within the Army. Many young soldiers became imbued with racist sentiments and with the notion that war was the climax of human existence. This took a major indoctrinational effort.[133]

The propaganda included pseudo-religious images portraying

---

132 Westermann, pp. 59 and 234.
133 Omer Bartov. *Hitler's Army: Soldiers, Nazis, and War in the Third Reich.* New York: Oxford University Press, 1992, pp. 106–115.

Hitler and the Nazi creed as God's instruments charged with protecting German culture and blood and showing Communism as Satan's servant, unleashed from hell to destroy civilization.[134] In addition to the ideological component, Bartov cites other mechanisms effectively utilized by the *Wehrmacht* in building a disciplined killing machine. The harsh discipline imposed by the German Army prevented disintegration. A strong identity with the Army as an extension of the German people, combined with a fanatic belief that their cause was just, made the *Wehrmacht* an extraordinary army that fought well under almost primitive conditions on the eastern front.

Ideology may have played a major role in the Nazi atrocities of World War II, but it was by no means the only cause. Soldiers on both sides committed unspeakable crimes against each other and civilians, few of which had anything to do with ideology. The military leadership utilized all the techniques described by Grossman—emotional distance, dehumanization of the enemy, and a desire to obey orders—to overcome a soldier's natural reluctance to kill.

---

134 Bartov, p. 124.

CHAPTER 13
Military Justice

VIETNAM was something of a watershed for the prosecution of American soldiers for crimes against civilians. Murder, rape, robbery, and the mistreatment of prisoners were by far the most common offenses for which soldiers faced court-martial. The number of prosecutions increased after My Lai. This was no doubt a reaction to the vigorous press coverage of the Calley trial and the public perception of the war effort.

To some historians, many soldiers sent to Vietnam were set up to fail. To begin with, 80 percent had little better than a high school education. High school dropouts were three times more likely than college graduates to be in combat.[135] US soldiers in Vietnam averaged nineteen years of age, compared to twenty-two in World War II. Additionally, 25 percent came from poor families, 55 percent from working-class homes, and 20 percent from middle-class backgrounds.[136]

Enlistment standards were low, as well. In 1965 the military began

135 Allison, p. 29.
136 Allison, p. 29.

accepting a higher percentage of applicants who scored in the two lowest categories of the mental examination required for enlistment. Many of these enlistees, who had low intelligence quotients, came from poor and broken homes. Adding to this mix was the McNamara 100,000, a program designed by Secretary of Defense Robert McNamara to give young men from inner cities and rural areas with extremely low examination scores a chance to grow and develop skills through military service. It didn't turn out well. In all, 240,000 men were accepted into the military under this program; 6 percent received some technical training, getting their reading skills up to the fifth-grade level. Overall, 40 percent of McNamara inductees were trained for combat as opposed to only 25 percent of all inductees, and one-half of the McNamara inductees were sent to Vietnam. The death rate for these men was twice that of the overall rate for US forces. By lowering the standards for induction the military had created conditions where discipline would be a problem.[137]

Lack of discipline and poor leadership were two critical components of the My Lai and Son Thang incidents. The breakdown of discipline reflected the military's poor job of training these soldiers to perform under adverse conditions. Training should make action instinctive; reinforcement of training is critical to maintaining battlefield discipline and combat readiness. Clear communication of the rules of engagement was sorely lacking in both these incidents. Medina and Ambort both improperly conveyed the message that avenging fallen comrades by "getting some" implied that the murder of innocents was acceptable.

Control of subordinates is essential to preventing atrocities and maintaining combat readiness. In both these incidents the officers failed to control their men, and in the case of Calley an officer actively

---

137 Allison, pp. 29–30.

participated in the killing. Medina's claim that he was unaware of the killing is not persuasive since he was nearby, was in radio contact with his platoons at all times, and heard the shooting, knowing full well there was no enemy return fire. Medina failed to control his subordinates, a colossal failure of leadership.

CHAPTER 14
Stepping on Ants

THE mechanisms for turning a soldier into a killer described by David Grossman were very much in evidence in the Vietnam massacres. The soldiers who participated in the killings were emotionally distant from their victims. This utter lack of empathy allows the person to overcome their natural resistance to killing. Erich Fromm called it a momentary emotional withdrawal that gives rise to destructive aggression.[138]

Probably the most significant mechanism was the cultural distance between the soldiers and the victims. Many American soldiers in Vietnam were notoriously disrespectful of the Vietnamese. Vietnamese were often referred to as "gooks," "slants," and "dinks." This cultural arrogance was exacerbated by the body count mentality that permeated the entire military command. One veteran said this permitted him to think that killing the NVA and Viet Cong was like "stepping on ants."[139]

While many American soldiers appreciated the Vietnamese culture, others were often isolated and felt that the Vietnamese they

138 Grossman, p. 160.
139 Grossman, p. 161.

saw were only ever trying to kill them. This gave rise to suspicion and hatred. One veteran said that to him the Vietnamese "were less than animals."[140] This cultural distance was not unique to Vietnam. Adolph Hitler convinced most Germans in World War II that they were the superior race and that the war was being fought to preserve and promote the Aryan master race.

Racism was clearly a contributing factor in the My Lai and Son Thang atrocities. The cultural distance was part of the desensitization process that military trainers used to train soldiers to kill. It is much easier to kill someone if they look distinctly different from you. If your propaganda machine can convince your soldiers that their opponents are not really human but are "inferior forms of life," then their natural reluctance to killing will be reduced.[141]

American appeals to racial superiority were not unique to Vietnam. During World War II, the Allies often used racist code words and imagery to advance their cause. For example, they constantly referred to the Japanese as "subhuman," often turning to images of apes and vermin to convey this.[142] Ernie Pyle, the famous American war correspondent, wrote, "In Europe we felt our enemies, horrible and deadly as they were, were still people. But out here I soon gathered that the Japanese were looked upon as something subhuman and repulsive; the way some people feel about cockroaches or mice."[143]

Another glaring example of racial stigmatization was the massive incarceration of Japanese-Americans in 1942. Hundreds of thousands of Japanese-Americans were relocated to internment camps for the duration of the war. Many, if not most, were American citizens, yet they

---

140 Grossman, pp. 162–163.

141 Grossman, p. 161.

142 John W. Dower. *War Without Mercy: Race and Power in the Pacific War.* New York: Pantheon Books, 1986, p. 9.

143 Dower, p. 78.

were deprived of due process and treated like criminals without any basis other than their Japanese heritage. This official sanction of racial stigma exacerbated anti-Japanese sentiment in the United States.[144]

References to the Japanese as "nips," "Japs," and "gooks" became part of the racial slang commonly used during World War II.[145] John Dower makes a compelling argument that the historic American fears of the "yellow peril" dating back to the nineteenth century remained pervasive. By 1940, a revolution was taking place in military technology and strategy, giving the Allied powers—among other things—the flamethrower, the B-29 super fortress bomber, napalm, the tactic of strategic bombing, the identification of civilian morale as an important and legitimate target in war, the tactical perfection of low-level saturation bombing raids over urban centers, and finally, nuclear weapons. Over the course of the war in Asia, racism, dehumanization, technological change, and exterminationist policies became interlocked in unprecedented ways.[146]

Twenty years later the United States became mired in a war in Southeast Asia against another Asian foe that seemed equally difficult to defeat. Racist attitudes do not dissipate quickly. The young soldiers fighting in Vietnam were no doubt influenced by the views of their parents, many of whom most likely fought in World War II. Additionally, the military leadership was heavily influenced by the experiences of World War II and could not avoid passing their prejudices on to their recruits. Racism may not have been actively encouraged by the military, but it was part of the cultural baggage Americans brought with them to Vietnam. At many levels it persisted, and the military did little to

---

144 Dower, p. 80.
145 Dower, p. 81.
146 Dower, p. 93.

eradicate it. Among the many factors contributing to the massacres, racism was certainly an important one.

The other factor that played a significant role was many of the men's belief that they were following orders combined with their desire to follow orders. As Milgram pointed out from his experiments, there is often a strong need to obey authority. The military culture in particular places a great emphasis on following orders. Questioning the orders of a superior officer is not encouraged and, in fact, can be fatal to one's military career.

After Son Thang, Boyd and Green both testified that they fired in response to Randy Herrod's orders to kill all the women and children. Following My Lai, Calley testified that his participation in the killings was a direct response to Captain Medina's order to kill everyone in the village. Private Meadlo and others also testified that they fired into the crowds of women and children because they were ordered to do so by their superior officer, Lieutenant Calley. Milgram reminds us: "Never underestimate the power of the need to obey."[147]

Of course, following orders as a defense to military atrocities was nullified at Nuremburg; however, given the nature of the individuals and the circumstances surrounding these incidents it is sadly plausible that these soldiers actually believed they were doing the right thing.

---

147 Grossman, p. 142.

CHAPTER 15
Why?

HISTORIANS, writers, military scholars, and psychologists have wrestled with the question of why these men committed these crimes and who is ultimately responsible for these horrific events. This remains one of the great mysteries of My Lai and Son Thang. Tim O'Brien, noted author and Vietnam veteran, poses the question: why did these guys do it, and not others?[148] Is that the ultimate mystery of evil, or is there a more basic response? How do we explain the depravity of Calley and Herrod and the heroism of Hugh Thompson and Ron Ridenhour? Is it enough to simply write these events off as battlefield frenzy or combat fatigue that sapped their participants of their judgment and reset their moral compasses?

Martin Gershen asserts that "there was no massacre of innocent civilians in My Lai on March 16, 1968. What happened there was a terribly unfortunate accident of war. It was less serious than the human or mechanical error that causes an artilleryman to fire a round so short it kills friendly troops. We allow for human error and

---

148 Anderson, p. 174.

malfunctioning machinery. When will we accept the fact that human minds sometimes go awry too?" Ultimately Gershen concludes that bad Army intelligence, faulty leadership, inadequate troop indoctrination, poor judgment, and a questionable counter-guerrilla policy caused My Lai.[149] Army policy was to kill, kill, kill and burn, burn, burn. With that as a policy Gershen sees atrocities as an inevitable by-product of a misguided military effort.

Ron Ridenhour also offers more sympathy than blame. To him the perpetrators were impressionable and scared and were "following orders in a context in which they'd been trained to follow orders." He saw the military command and the "architects of the policy" as the ones who should have been put on trial, the people who had created the Vietnam strategy and should have known where it would lead.[150]

Richard Hammer offers some support for this theory. Among the Americans there was little understanding of the problems facing the Vietnamese. Americans acted only under the assumption that any Vietnamese who lived in a free-fire zone, who lived in a contested area, was automatically a Viet Cong and was, therefore, fair game. No distinction was made between friend and foe. With such elements and such attitudes a Son Thang was inevitable.[151]

These views were consistent with most of the antiwar proponents at the time. Seymour Hersh quoting Herbert Carter—the one and only American casualty of the My Lai massacre, who shot himself in the foot to avoid participation in the carnage—said, "What happened at My Lai was not a massacre but a logical result of the war in Vietnam. The people didn't know what they were dying for and the guys didn't know why they were shooting them."[152]

---

149   Gershen, pp. 301–302.
150   Bilton and Sim, p. 362.
151   Hammer, pp. 201–202.
152   Hersh, p. 84.

Guenter Lewy sees those excuses as a repudiation of individual responsibility, not unlike those made with regard to the German people after World War II. He aptly points out that guilt is personal and collective guilt has no place in our jurisprudence. It is easy to blame the entire military for the actions of a few. Some individuals under pressure and sometimes provocation have committed atrocities, while others have successfully resisted these pressures and maintained their integrity. Instead of facing the harsh fact of individual moral failure it was easier for opponents of the war to place the blame on the backs of the generals.[153]

President Richard M. Nixon, sensing a political disaster and a significant blow to public support for the war, wrote in his memoirs, "Calley's crime was inexcusable. But many of the Congressmen and commentators who expressed outrage about My Lai were not really as interested in the moral questions raised by Calley as they were in using the incident to make political attacks against the war." He went on to say that he thought "most Americans understood that the My Lai massacre was not representative of our people, of the war we were fighting, or of our men who were fighting it; but from the time it became public the whole tragic episode was used by the media and the antiwar forces to chip away at our efforts to build public support for our Vietnam objectives and policies."[154]

In reference to the Son Thang massacre, Gary Solis felt the strong bond formed among Marines, which emphasizes a fierce loyalty to fellow Marines, obscured their judgment. They shared the Marine tradition of ethos, which placed a high priority on obedience. In addition the

---

153   Guenter Lewy. *America in Vietnam.* New York: Oxford University Press, 1978, pp. 315–316.
154   Olson and Roberts, pp. 192–193.

relative safety of the group, thus diffusing personal responsibility, made killing that much easier.[155]

Commenting on My Lai in terms that apply to Son Thang, Michael Walzer wrote: "It has been argued on behalf of these soldiers that they acted, not in the heat of battle (since there was no battle) but in the context of a brutal and brutalizing war … They had been encouraged to kill without making careful discriminations—encouraged to do so by their own officers and driven to it by their enemies, who fought and hid among the civilian population. These statements are true, or partly true; and yet massacre is radically different from guerilla war … This was not a fearful and frenzied extension of combat, but 'free' and systematic slaughter, and the men who participated in it can hardly say that they were caught in the grip of war."[156]

Those who blame the military and the failed policies make a strong argument. The war was badly managed. There were no clear military objectives. The metric for success was body counts—a metric that skewed and muddied the actual success of the war effort. The policy of rapid troop rotation or turnaround was devastating to unit cohesiveness and camaraderie, elements that are critical for military success. There were too many men moving in and out of units, looking only to survive the twelve-month rotation. Additionally, the pervasive cultural arrogance and disregard for the Vietnamese contributed to a climate of hostility, fear, and suspicion. That the war was a guerrilla war, a type of fighting for which American troops were ill trained, added to the frustration and deterioration in morale. Lastly, the racial problems and rampant drug use only exacerbated an already volatile situation.

However, none of that provides adequate justification for the atrocities that took place. Ultimately, those who participated in the

155 Solis, p. 309.
156 Solis, p. 310.

carnage bear responsibility for their actions. Why did some participate and others not? Why were some repulsed by the actions of their comrades, and why did they refuse to follow orders to kill? Clearly some simply saw the actions for what they were: mass killing of innocent civilians on a large scale with no military purpose whatsoever.

Charlie Company and the Seventh Marine Battalion were not the only units in Vietnam to suffer casualties at the hands of the enemy. Snipers, sappers, booby traps, and mines were a way of life in Vietnam. Every American combat unit incurred casualties of that nature in the war. Not all of them engaged in cold-blooded murder. Ultimately, each individual soldier had to make a choice that day as he did every day. Whether they were weak like Meadlo and Green or strong like Calley and Herrod, they made the same wrong choice. Whatever the makeup of their personalities, they had to choose. They were not in danger, there was no threat, and there was no enemy present. Venting anger and frustration is no excuse for murdering, raping, and mutilating innocent women and children. These were not split-second decisions made in the heat of battle. These were measured, premeditated, and deliberate, with malice aforethought. They were crimes committed by United States service personnel who were not prosecuted to the fullest extent of the law. As O'Brien points out in Anderson's book on My Lai: "They are confessed murderers. If I were a prosecutor I would try to find some way to bring these people to account for murder."[157]

The mystery of My Lai and Son Thang may be that we will never know what triggered the madness the men exhibited during those atrocities. The pressure to enhance body counts, the desire to avenge fallen comrades, the frustration of being victimized by a poorly executed guerilla war, poor leadership, and the racist attitudes of the Americans

---

157   Anderson, p. 176.

toward the Vietnamese all contributed to a perfect storm of violent behavior.

However, there is a difference between wanting to exact revenge and actually doing it. The difference in these situations is that the men who committed these murders thought they would get away with them. Whether because they believed they were following orders or because they were acting in concert with a group, they believed there would be no consequences for their actions. During their tours of duty they had witnessed numerous acts of extraordinary cruelty toward the Vietnamese people. Not only had they become desensitized to the heinous nature of their actions, but they learned that there would be no adverse consequences as a result. My Lai and Son Thang were extensions of what they had been witnessing for years, just on a much grander scale. Whatever moral code would normally inhibit individuals from committing murder was overwhelmed by the rage and hatred these men felt. The belief that their actions would have no adverse consequences only added to the madness. Sadly, many of them were right; there were no consequences for them.

No doubt many of those who participated in the killings have lived with terrible guilt and anxiety about what they did more than forty years ago in Vietnam. Varnado Simpson describes his ordeal: "I have an image of it in my mind every night, every day. I have nightmares. I constantly have nightmares of the children or someone. I can see the people. I can go somewhere and see a face that reminds me of the people that I killed. I can see that vividly, just like it happened today, right now."[158]

While many may reside in their own private hell others have found a way to rationalize what happened and move on. Randy Herrod was awarded his Silver Star and returned home a hero.

---

158 Bilton and Sim, p. 8.

CHAPTER 16
New Rules

MAJOR General Ronald Griffith's exhortation to his men on the eve of the first Gulf War is an indication of how the atrocities in Vietnam—in particular, My Lai—have affected military thinking since 1970. Eckhardt describes some of the improvements in military training that are a direct result of the military's experience in Vietnam.

Battlefield misconduct: Misconduct is caused by a lack of discipline. The military went back to emphasizing basic military principles.

Professional training: Being a soldier requires constant training. A soldier must be able to perform skills in harmony with others.

Compliance with standard operating procedure: Collective training leads to an agreed-upon way of acting in a given situation. Training makes correct action instinctive.

Compliance with the rules of engagement: Rules of engagement tell soldiers when and under what circumstances they may shoot. The entire chain of command must know, understand, and enforce those rules.

Control of subordinates: A responsible commander is what legally and practically distinguishes an armed force from rabble. My Lai taught us the necessity of clear, concise, legal orders. Every superior officer must intervene at the first sign of lack of discipline.

Insistence on the truthful, moral "high road": Whenever force is used, three questions must be answered in the affirmative: Is it legal? Is it moral? Does it make common sense? Only if these questions can be answered in the affirmative should an order be given to fire. Train, expect, and demand the highest ethical conduct from those who employ force.[159]

My Lai and Son Thang also brought the return of the law of war into military training. In 1972 the Department of Defense directed that an overall law of war program be established to define training standards for all people. In addition the law of war was made a command responsibility. It is now expressly taught that soldiers must protect the innocent and are not to unnecessarily kill noncombatants. The International Red Cross has said the United States has the best law of war training program in the world.[160]

In addition, computer technology and renewed emphasis on professional battlefield behavior have produced remarkable progress on rules of engagement. The law took its appropriate place in the battle staff. Now senior combat commanders have active staff cells that draft mission-specific rules of engagement at the same time as war plans are being made for troops, logistics, and operations. Control of force and protecting the lives of both soldiers and noncombatants are the goals.[161]

Another important lesson is that of increased communication

---

159   Eckhardt, pp. 19–20.
160   Anderson, p. 164.
161   Eckhardt, p. 21.

between the military, the civilian command, and the public. Force must only be used in pursuit of policy objectives that are clearly articulated. In any democracy communication is critical to ensure appropriate public support for the military objective.[162]

Since Vietnam, the US military has undergone significant changes. The draft was abolished and replaced with an all-volunteer military. This has resulted in a better motivated and better educated fighting force.

Next, radical upgrades in the armed forces during the Reagan administration elevated the level of training and the quality of equipment. Advances in technology, both military and medical, have given American forces a distinct advantage in military combat. More accurate long-range weapons, the use of drones and robotic devices, new Kevlar vests, and improved battlefield medical equipment have dramatically enhanced the combat effectiveness of American service personnel. A greater emphasis on force protection and improved training for counterinsurgency have resulted in substantially reduced casualties and greater survivability for wounded soldiers.

The cultural arrogance associated with the atrocities in Vietnam has been eradicated from current training techniques. There is now a greater emphasis on teaching combat troops to respect local customs and values. There is a greater emphasis on "winning hearts and minds" as opposed to brute military force. The United States and its allies are quick to offer apologies and to provide financial compensation to families of innocents accidentally killed or wounded by allied forces. The rules of engagement are clear and often slanted toward protecting civilian populations, even sometimes at the risk of exposing allied forces to enemy fire.

Wartime objectives are articulated better in present days. President

---

162 Eckhardt, pp. 22–23.

George H. W. Bush established the liberation of Kuwait as the only policy goal of Gulf War I, which allowed Saddam Hussein to remain in power, a decision that was criticized by many who felt the United States should have taken Baghdad and deposed Hussein. Further, President George W. Bush established the enforcement of UN sanctions as justification for the invasion of Iraq in 2003. Prior to that he and America's NATO allies invaded Afghanistan to topple the Taliban and eradicate Al-Qaeda in response to the 9/11 attacks on the United States. President Obama has similarly articulated his intent to increase American military troop commitments to Afghanistan in order to secure the country before bringing the troops out in 2011.

These new policies and training techniques have been tested in Iraq and Afghanistan. Afghanistan in particular has striking similarities to Vietnam. It is small and relatively primitive. Most of the population is illiterate. Most of them have little connection to the central government but have stronger ties to tribal or religious leaders. The central government under President Hamid Karzai is viewed as corrupt and ineffective. It is propped up by the United States and other European powers. The vast majority of the population is Muslim and generally disapproves of many American values and distrusts the United States. The country has a long history of repelling outside forces, and a country has never successfully occupied Afghanistan. The Taliban has proven to be a resilient and creative enemy, able to prevent the NATO alliance from achieving its military goals in spite of its overwhelming advantage in military firepower. Finally, also like Vietnam, winning the hearts and minds of the Afghan people has not been easy.

However, having learned the lessons of Vietnam, the United States has done a much better job of ensuring battlefield discipline, encouraging respect for the Afghan people, and articulating clear rules of engagement. In Iraq as well the difference in the American approach has been radically apparent, and Iraq may yet prove to be a success story as it tries to get its fledgling democracy off the ground.

These conflicts have not been without criminal incidents. The scandal of American mistreatment of Iraqi prisoners at Abu Ghraib and the murder of an Iraqi family at Haditha by a squad of Marines to cover up the rape of a fourteen-year-old girl are stark reminders of how the United States must be vigilant in its training and selection process.

Abu Ghraib in particular had striking parallels to My Lai as an example of what happens when there is a complete breakdown of command discipline. The inquiry into the abuses of Iraqi prisoners at Abu Ghraib found that the entire 800th Military Police Brigade was inadequately trained for its mission with "a general lack of knowledge, implementation, and emphasis of basic legal, regulatory, doctrinal and command requirements."[163] The soldiers were demoralized by their extended tour of duty in Iraq and were often under attack from insurgents. They felt overwhelmed by the magnitude of their mission. There were conflicting lines of responsibility between the military police, military intelligence, and CIA civilians who were interrogating the prisoners for information. Abu Ghraib housed seven thousand prisoners with only ninety-two military police guards to keep them under control.[164]

The official inquiry into Abu Ghraib found disorganization, inadequate leadership, and poor supervision, which worked to produce an attitude of fear and resentment among the guards. The post-9/11 treatment of prisoners as enemy combatants had blurred the line between the protocols set forth in the US Army Field Manual and

---

163   Steven Strasser. *The Abu Ghraib Investigations.* New York: Public Affairs, 2004, p. xii.

164   Strasser, p. xiv.

the enhanced interrogation techniques championed by the CIA.[165] Ultimately, the civilian leadership sets the policy. However, without a clear and consistent policy based upon sound legal principles, the potential for abuse will always exist.

The swift and firm response to these events and the public outrage are examples of how the post-My Lai military and American public have evolved. There was no sympathy for the perpetrators, and no indictment of the military or loss of support for the war effort was attributable to these specific incidents.

The twenty-four-hour nature of our modern news cycle has produced a more media-savvy and transparent military leadership. It is not uncommon for generals to be seen regularly on TV news shows and to be called to testify before Congress. These events help establish a better comfort level between the public and the military, which reduces the public distrust and skepticism regarding the military that characterized the Vietnam era.

Eckhardt summed up the lessons learned by describing how the former Communist countries of Eastern Europe looked to the West to reform their militaries. The doctrine that they seek to emulate has three essential components: civilian control of the military; respect for the rule of law, including the law of war; and respect for the rights of individual soldiers. This military doctrine was critical in the democratization of these new nations.[166]

---

165   Strasser, p. xvi.
166   Eckhardt, p. 27.

CONCLUSION

We may never know what really happened at My Lai and Son Thang. Whatever evil lurks in the hearts of men rose to the surface that day and exploded in a tempest of hate and rage. It was a perfect storm of hate, chaos, violence, rage, revenge, and opportunity.

Where do these atrocities fit in the historical context of Vietnam? Was it that these aberrations were a natural by-product of a policy conceived by military doctrine that was doomed to fail? One lesson Browning taught us is that ordinary men committed these crimes. Anyone is capable of committing mass murder under the right circumstances.

Americans have not fully come to grips with the Vietnam experience, so My Lai and Son Thang remain unresolved issues in the American memory. American soldiers committing mass murder does not comport with our commonly held views of American servicemen always being the good guys. The men who stormed the beaches on D-day and raised the American flag on Iwo Jima were not capable of murdering innocent women and children in cold blood. We are the ones fighting oppression and promoting freedom and democracy throughout the world.

Atrocities should never be forgotten, for once forgotten they no longer serve as a reminder of man's capacity for evil. The involuntary contribution of the victims at My Lai and Son Thang is the constant reminder that society must be vigilant in the use of military might. Americans must be aware of the human capacity to engage in unspeakable acts and then to rationalize them. The victims will hopefully serve as a constant reminder that America must never stop striving for a military that is comprised of soldiers who will always act like Hugh Thompson. The military must always reflect those values that make the United States a unique nation. So My Lai and Son Thang cannot be forgotten; as it is with the Holocaust, only by keeping the memory alive can we ensure the tragedy does not happen again.

The judicial process that adjudicated these crimes was unsatisfying. Unfortunately the process is far from perfect but has endured as a model forum for addressing war crimes committed by American troops. While many of those who engaged in the murder of innocent civilians at My Lai and Son Thang were not sent to jail, they must live with the knowledge of what they have done, which no doubt in some cases is quite painful.

Unfortunately these incidents force us to come to terms with our own failures as a nation and to fully comprehend the nature of our conduct during the Vietnam War. As Edwin Simmons, Director Emeritus of the Marine Corps History Museum, said: "Americans like to believe that atrocities are committed by others, but we are not immune from such things. We like to think we are, but we are not."[167]

---

167   Solis, p. xvi.

Appendix A

MACV

MILITARY ASSISTANCE COMMAND, VIETNAM

Pocket Card, "Nine Rules"

Rules: The Vietnamese have paid a heavy price in suffering for their long fight against the communists. We military men are in Vietnam now because their government has asked us to help its soldiers and people in winning their struggle. The Viet Cong will attempt to turn the Vietnamese people against you. You can defeat them at every turn by the strength, understanding, and generosity you display with the people. Here are nine simple rules:

1.) Remember we are guests here: We make no demands and seek no special treatment.

2.) Join with the people! Understand their life, use phrases from their language and honor their customs and laws.

3.) Treat women with politeness and respect.

4.) Make personal friends among the soldiers and common people.

5.) Always give the Vietnamese the right of way.

6.) Be alert to security and ready to react with your military skill.

7.) Don't attract attention by loud, rude or unusual behavior.

8.) Avoid separating yourself from the people by a display of wealth or privilege.

9.) Above all else you are members of the U.S. Military Forces on a difficult mission, responsible for all your official and personal actions. Reflect honor upon yourself and the United States of America.

DISTRIBUTION -- one to each member of the United States Armed Forces in Vietnam (September 1967).

MACV Pocket Card, "The Enemy In Your Hands"

As a member of the U.S. Military Forces, you will comply with the Geneva Prisoner of War Convention of 1949 to which your country adheres. Under these Conventions:

You can and will:

- Disarm your prisoner.
- Immediately search him thoroughly.
- Require him to be silent.
- Segregate him from other prisoners.
- Guard him carefully.
- Take him to the place designated by your commander.

You cannot and must not:

- Mistreat your prisoner.
- Humiliate or degrade him.
- Take any of his personal effects that do not have significant military value.
- Refuse him medical treatment if required and available.

ALWAYS TREAT YOUR PRISONER HUMANELY

KEY PHRASES

English	Vietnamese
Halt	Dung Lai
Lay down your gun	Buong sung xuong
Put up your hands	Dua tay len
Keep your hands on your head	Dau tay len dau

106

I will search you

Do not talk	Toi Kham ong
Turn Right	Lai dang kia
Turn Left	Xay ben phai
	Xay ben trai

THE ENEMY IN YOUR HANDS

1.) *Handle him firmly, promptly, but humanely.*

The captive must be disarmed, searched, secured and watched. But he must also be treated at all times as a human being. He must not be tortured, killed, mutilated, or degraded, even if he refuses to talk. If the captive is a woman, treat her with all respect due her sex.

2.) *Take the captive quickly to security.*

As soon as possible evacuate the captive to a place of safety and interrogation designated by your commander. Military documents taken from the captive are also sent to the interrogators, but the captive will keep his personal equipment except weapons.

3.) *Mistreatment of any captive is a criminal offense. Every soldier is personally responsible for the enemy in his hands.*

It is both dishonorable and foolish to mistreat a captive. It is also a punishable offense. Not even a beaten enemy will surrender if he knows his captors will torture or kill him. He will resist and make his capture more costly. Fair treatment of captives encourages the enemy to surrender.

4.) *Treat the sick and wounded captive as best you can.*

The captive saved may be an intelligence source. In any case he is a human being and must be treated like one. The soldier who ignores the sick and wounded degrades his uniform.

5.) *All persons in your hands, whether suspects, civilians, or combat captives, must be protected against violence, insults, curiosity, and reprisals of any kind.*

Leave punishment to the courts and judges. The soldier shows his strength by his fairness and humanity to the persons in his hands.

(September 1967)

MACV Pocket Card, "Guidance for Commanders in Vietnam"

1.) Make the welfare of your men your primary concern with special attention to mess, mail, and medical care.

2.) Give priority emphasis to matters of intelligence, counter-intelligence, and timely and accurate reporting.

3.) Gear your command for sustained operations: keep constant pressure on the enemy.

4.) React rapidly with all force available to opportunities to destroy the enemy; disrupt enemy bases, capturing or destroying his supply caches.

5.) Open up methodically and use roads, waterways, and the railroad; be alert and prepared to ambush the ambusher.

6.) Harass enemy lines of communication by raids and ambushes.

7.) Use your firepower with care and discrimination, particularly in populated areas.

8.) Capitalize on psywar opportunities.

9.) Assist in "revolutionary development" with emphasis on priority areas and on civic action wherever feasible.

10.) Encourage and help Vietnamese military and paramilitary units; involve them in your operations at every opportunity.

11.) Be smarter and more skillful than the enemy; stimulate professionalism, alertness and tactical ingenuity; seize every opportunity to enhance training of men and units.

12.) Keep your officers and men well informed, aware of the nine rule for personnel of MACV, and mindful of the techniques of communist insurgency and the role of free world forces in Vietnam.

13.) Maintain an alert "open door" policy on complaints and sensitivity to detection and correction of malpractice.

14.)   Recognize bravery and outstanding work.

15.)   Inspect frequently units two echelons below your level in insure
        compliance with the foregoing.

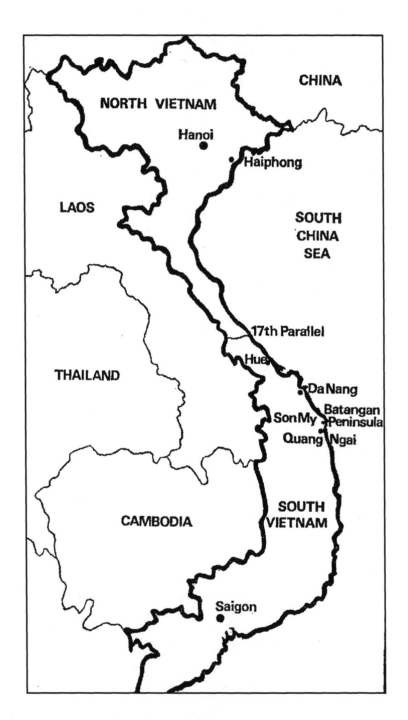

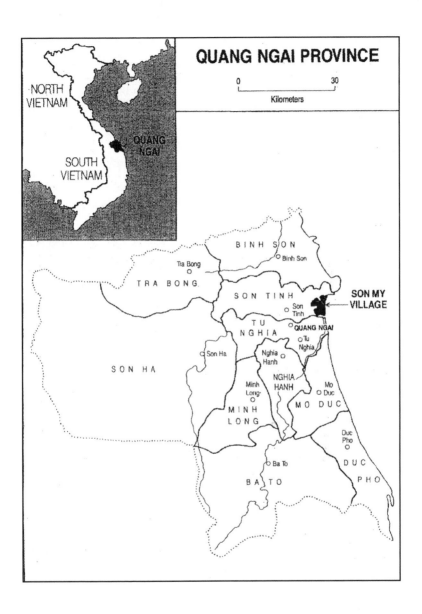

QUANG NGAI PROVINCE

0 ——————————— 30

Kilometers

NORTH VIETNAM

SOUTH VIETNAM

QUANG NGAI

BINH SON

○ Binh Son

Tra Bong ○

TRA BONG

SON TINH

Son Tinh ○

SON MY VILLAGE

QUANG NGAI

TU NGHIA

○ Tu Nghia

Son Ha ○

SON HA

Nghia Hanh ○

NGHIA HANH

Minh Long ○

MINH LONG

MO DUC

Mo Duc ○

Duc Pho ○

Ba To ○

BA TO

DUC PHO

111

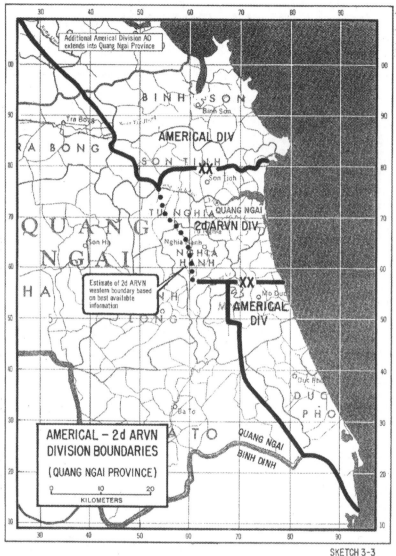

Additional Americal Division AO extends into Quang Ngai Province

AMERICAL DIV

XX

2d ARVN DIV

Estimate of 2d ARVN western boundary based on best available information

XX

AMERICAL DIV

AMERICAL – 2d ARVN
DIVISION BOUNDARIES

(QUANG NGAI PROVINCE)

0   10   20
KILOMETERS

SKETCH 3-3

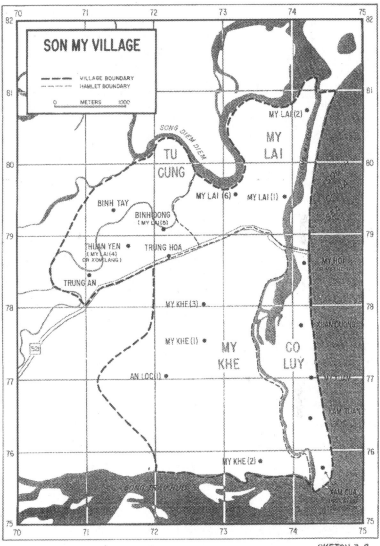

SKETCH 3-2

A member of the patrol from 1st Battalion, 7th Marines which investigated allegations of murder in Son Thang (4). He stands on the "patio" where six women and children died.

This photograph was Article 32 investigative exhibit 15. Marine investigators examine the Son Thang (4) hut where four Vietnamese women and children were murdered.

"Open up! Kill them all, kill all of them!" Six women and children died in front of this hut.

This was investigative exhibit number 23 from the Article 32 investigation of events that occurred in Son Thang (4). Huts 1, 2, and 3 mark where the Vietnamese victims died.

BIBLIOGRAPHY

Allison, William T. *Military Justice in Vietnam: The Rule of Law in an American War.* Lawrence, Kansas: University Press of Kansas, 2007.

Anderson, David L. *Facing My Lai: Moving Beyond the Massacre.* Lawrence, Kansas: University Press of Kansas, 1998.

Bartov, Omer. *Hitler's Army: Soldiers, Nazis, and War in the Third Reich.* New York: Oxford University Press, 1992.

Belknap, Michal R. *The Vietnam War on Trial: The My Lai Massacre and the Court-Martial of Lieutenant Calley.* Lawrence, Kansas: University Press of Kansas, 2002.

Bilton, Michael and Kevin Sim. *Four Hours in My Lai.* New York: Viking, 1971.

Browning, Christopher. *Ordinary Men: Reserve Police Battalion 101 and the Final Solution in Poland.* New York: HarperCollins, 1992.

Dower, John W. *War Without Mercy: Race and Power in the Pacific War.* New York: Pantheon Books, 1986

Fitzgerald, Frances. *Fire in the Lake: The Vietnamese and the Americans in Vietnam*. Boston: Little, Brown and Company, 1972.

Garrison, Denzil D. *Honor Restored*. Mustang, Oklahoma: Tate Publishing, 2006.

Gershen, Martin. *Destroy or Die: The True Story of My Lai*. New Rochelle, New York: Arlington House, 1971.

Goldhagen, Daniel J. *Hitler's Willing Executioners: Ordinary Germans and the Holocaust*. New York: Vintage Books, 1996.

Goldstein, Joseph, Burke Marshall, and Jack Schwartz. *The My Lai Massacre and Its Cover-Up: Beyond the Reach of Law? The Peers Commission Report*. New York: The Free Press, 1976.

Grossman, David. *On Killing: The Psychological Cost of Learning to Kill in War and Society*. Boston: Little, Brown and Company, 1995.

Hammer, Richard. *One Morning in the War: The Tragedy at Son My*. New York: Coward-McCann, 1970.

Herrod, Randy. *Blue's Bastards: A True Story of Valor Under Fire*. Washington, DC: Regnery Publishing, 1989.

Hersh, Seymour M. *My Lai 4: A Report on the Massacre and Its Aftermath*. New York: Random House, 1970.

Lewy, Guenter. *America in Vietnam*. New York: Oxford University Press, 1978.

O'Brien, Tim. *The Things They Carried*. New York: Mariner Books, 1990.

Oliver, Kendrick. *The My Lai Massacre in American History and Memory.* Manchester, UK: Manchester University Press, 2006.

Olson, James S. and Randy Roberts. *My Lai: A Brief History with Documents.* New York: Bedford Books, 1998.

Solis, Gary D. *Son Thang: An American War Crime.* New York: Bantam Books, 1997.

Strasser, Steven. *The Abu Ghraib Investigations.* New York: Public Affairs, 2004.

Trial transcripts of the court-martial of William Calley. Edwin Moïse bibliography of My Lai: www.clemson.edu/caah/history /facultypages/ edmoise/mylai.html.

Trial transcripts of the trial of Ernest Medina. Edwin Moïse bibliography of My Lai: www.clemson.edu/caah/history/facultypages/edmoise /mylai.html.

Uniform Code of Military Justice. Accessible online at www.au.af.mil /au/awc/awcgate/ucmj.

Westermann, Edward B. *Hitler's Police Battalions: Enforcing Racial War in the East.* Lawrence, Kansas: University Press of Kansas, 2005.

INDEX

Page numbers with *italic* "*n*" indicates a reference in the footnote

Page numbers with *italic* "*ill*" indicates a reference to illustrations, drawings or photographs

121

arriving at Landing Zone Dottie, 26
reports of VC activities in, 24
T'Souvas, Robert, 48
Turner, Thomas, 40

U

Uniform Code of Military Justice,
Article 118, conditions where soldiers
can be charged with murder, 36, 36*n*
United States Army Field Manual, 36
United States (US)
after Tet Offensive, xii–xiii
American opinion about Calley,
75–76
casualties (1968) of war in Vietnam,
xii
forces in Son My, 17
rise as world power, xi
in Somalia, 11–12
*United States v. Captain Ernest L.
Medina*, prosecution brief on the Law
of Principals in, 44*n*
US Army
changes in since My Lai, 49–50
Charlie Company, 18–23
mistreatment of Iraqi prisoners at
Abu Ghraib, 101–102
reports of VC activities in My Lai, 24
US Army Field Manual, Iraqi prisoners
at Abu Ghraib and, 101–102
US Army Rangers, in Somalia, 11–12
US Department of Defense,
establishment of law of war program,
98
US Marines
attack on My Lai, 27–30
killing of Iraqi family at Haditha,
101
killings at Son Thang, xiii, 57–59
number stationed around Danang,
51
in Que Son, 52–53

V

veterans, reactions to gruesomeness of
killing, 5
Viet Cong (VC)
around Danang, 51
formation of, 15
in Quang Ngai province, 21
regiments across Que Son, 52–53
reports of activities in My Lai, 24
soldiers definition of, 77
soldiers names for, 87
in Son Thang4, 54
stationed around Danang, 51
taking control of Son My, 16
Tet Offensive, xii
Viet Minh government, 15
Vietnam
ancestor worship in, 14
basic training focus for, 9–11
compared to Afghanistan, 100–101
impact of Calley verdict on war in,
46–50
impact outside world on, 14–15
management of war in, 94
map of, 110*ill*
partitioning of, 15
peoples view of rulers, 16
as watershed for prosecution of
American soldiers, 84–86
under wing of China, 14
The Vietnam War on Trial (Belknap), 18*n*

W

Walzer, Michael, 94
"war trophies," 49
War Without Mercy (Dower), 88*n*
wartime objectives, 99–100
Watergate scandal, 49
Watke, Frederick W., 32, 48–49
Webb, James H., Jr., 74
Wehrmacht, concept of, 82, 83
Weinberg, Gerhard, 10
Westermann, Edward B., 10, 81–82
Whitmore, Richard, 54
Williams, Robert C., 69
Willingham, Thomas K., 49